FIND OUT ABOUT
SECRET
CODES
AND MESSAGES

George Beal

**Illustrated by Jenny Thorne
and Oxford Illustrators Limited**

TREASURE PRESS

First published in Great Britain in 1973 by
The Hamlyn Publishing Group Limited
under the title *Codes, Ciphers and Secret Writing*.

This edition published in 1990 by
Treasure Press
Michelin House
81 Fulham Road
London SW3 6RB

ISBN 1 85051 605 7

Printed in Czechoslovakia
50768

Contents

Code or Cipher?

Ask any of your friends what they think a code is and the chances are that they will answer that it is a secret way of sending messages. In fact, not all codes are secret, nor are they all intended to be. A code is simply a convenient way of conveying information by any means at all.

Our ordinary language, whether written or spoken, is a type of code which is understood only by someone else in the possession of the right key. British and other people can speak and write English, so they are all holders of that important key—understanding. On the other hand, there are millions of people who do not understand a word of English. They are as unfamiliar with the English code, as most speakers of English are to other language codes.

Nearly all animals have ways of communicating with each other, either by sound or by some system of signalling. An elephant trumpets his message across the jungle, a dog barks or howls, and bees in a hive perform a kind of dance to 'tell' each other where nectar may be found. All are types of code, understood only by those who have learned, or inherited, the system used.

Writing is another form of code which can only be read by those who have learned not only the code of the language it is written in, but also the letters of the Latin alphabet 'code', and the numbers used for writing down amounts of money, dates, and mathematical calculations. Yet anyone who has collected stamps will know that the Latin alphabet is not the only one in use, even in Europe, and that there are many number systems.

Russian, Bulgarian, Jugoslavian and Greek stamps use letters from alphabets unfamiliar to most other Europeans, so that before the messages on the stamps can be read, those other alphabets have to be learned.

1	2	3	4	5	6	7	8	9	0	Modern European
١	٢	٣	٤	٥	٦	٧	٨	٩	٠	Modern Arabic
٩	٢	٤	٨	५	५	٦	८	९	٥	Tenth Century Indian
١	٢	٣	٤	٤	٥	٦	٧	٨		Twelfth Century Arabic
١	٢	٣	٤	٥	٦	٧	٨	٩	٥	Twelfth Century European
1	2	3	4	5	6	7	8	9	٥	Fourteenth Century European

Egyptian Writing

Nowadays, everyone knows that the inscriptions on the tombs and monuments of ancient Egypt are really messages, telling a story in a picture-system of writing. But only a couple of hundred years ago, no one could read them at all, and in fact there were many archaeologists who believed that the inscriptions had no strict meaning but were simply a kind of mystic, decorative pattern.

It may seem unlikely that the ancient Egyptian scribes who painted and carved the inscriptions on the tombs were employing any kind of code or cipher. Yet, really, this is what they were doing. In the days of the Pharaohs, the great bulk of the people could not read or write, and the mystic symbols had meaning only for certain scribes, priests and rulers.

After the collapse of the great ancient Egyptian empire, no one else could read the inscriptions either, although, over the centuries, many people had tried to decipher the hieroglyphics, as they were called. Experts were completely baffled, since they did not have the key to the 'code'.

The story of the decipherment of the Egyptian writings began in the year 1799, when an Egyptian workman, employed on building work by the French Army, discovered a flat, carved slab of black stone at a small town in Egypt called Rosetta. The workman took it to a French officer named Boussard, who was greatly intrigued by the strange symbols and signs which covered the stone. However, they meant nothing to him, so he reported what he had found, and the stone was removed to Cairo.

The piece of black stone was dubbed the 'Rosetta Stone', and French scholars quickly realised that there was something rather unusual about it. The Rosetta Stone, in fact, was written in three different alphabets or scripts: the top one was the familiar, but puzzling, Egyptian hieroglyphics, the middle one was written in *Demotic*, a simplified version of the picture script, while the last section was written in Greek.

Greek, of course, was a known language, and it seemed fairly obvious that the Stone contained the same message written in three different ways. Scholars realised that the vital key to the hitherto unknown Egyptian writing now lay in their hands, yet many years were to pass before anyone was able to solve the age-old problem of the hieroglyphics.

The Greek inscription was translated, and scholars compared it with the Egyptian, but drew a blank, except that some people suspected that ancient Egyptian might resemble the Coptic language, which is still spoken in Egypt by a small sect of Christians.

Egypt passed from French hands to the British, and in 1814, the Rosetta Stone was examined by Doctor Thomas Young, who knew most of the languages used in the Middle East, including Coptic. He knew, too, that other scholars had remarked upon the fact that many words in the Egyptian were enclosed in oval shapes, known as cartouches. A Danish scholar had guessed that these were probably Royal names or titles, so Young checked through the Greek for some names of this type. He settled upon 'Ptolemy', the name of one of the Pharaohs.

Now 'Ptolemy' is spelled a little differently in Greek, and looks like

Πτολεμαῖος, or *Ptolemaios*. When Young looked at what he thought was the Egyptian equivalent of the name, he saw an oval, or cartouche like the one below.

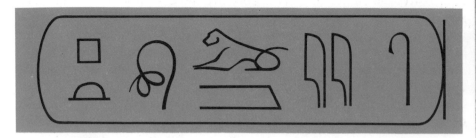

Doctor Young carefully wrote in what he thought were the equivalent sounds against the Egyptian characters:

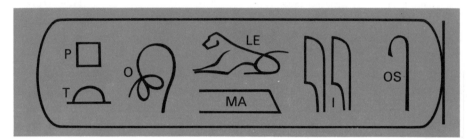

The doctor then wrote a long report on what he had found, and how it compared with other Egyptian inscriptions. His work was taken up by a young Frenchman named Jean-François Champollion. An obelisk, or stone monument, had recently been discovered in Egypt, and this also contained the name Ptolemy, and very helpfully, had an additional inscription in Greek. Here, Champollion came across another familiar name: Cleopatra, so he decided to seek out the equivalent in the Egyptian writing. At last, he hit upon a cartouche which looked like the one here.

In Greek, Cleopatra is written Κλεοπατρα (Kleopatra). Champollion numbered the Egyptian characters for easy reference, and assumed that the first symbol was 'K'. The next symbol he had already decided was 'L' from his work on the name Ptolemy. This gave him KL. He had previously guessed that the next two symbols were 'I' and 'O'. He now had KLIO. The fifth symbol had appeared in PTOLEMY as P, but symbols 6, 7, 8, 9 and 10 were unknown. Champollion guessed that since 6 and 9 were the same, they must represent A. So he now had the following:

> K L I O P A . . A . .
> 1 2 3 4 5 6 7 8 9 10 11

Cleopatra

Champollion further guessed symbols 7 and 8 were 'T' and 'R', giving KLIOPATRA, whilst the last two probably indicated that the subject concerned was a Royal person. He then discovered that symbol 3 could mean both E and I, and by working through this system, he was able to work out the phonetic values, or sounds, of the other Egyptian symbols.

Of course, the language itself was strange, too, but Champollion, knowing Coptic, was able to piece together the rest of the inscription on the Rosetta Stone. Using the knowledge he had gained, Champollion was then able to go on to other inscriptions, and in this way, the whole of the Egyptian writings were deciphered.

Minoan Scripts

A similar story applies to the script found in the ancient remains on the island of Crete. Arthur Evans, a young archaeologist, began excavations there in 1900 on what proved to be the ruins of a great civilisation, once ruled over by the legendary King Minos. Yet the writings found by Evans were not in any known alphabet, and despite years of hard work by Evans himself, and others afterwards, they were only able to discover that the language was a form of Greek, using a different alphabet.

Scholars worked on, but the man who really deciphered the Minoan inscriptions was Michael Ventris, who had followed in the footsteps of another hard-working decipherer, Alice Kober. Unlike the case of the Egyptian hieroglyphics, the Minoan scripts had no Rosetta Stone, or key, and breaking the code was simply a matter of very hard work.

Runes

There are many other inscriptions which have never been deciphered, although the majority of the better-known scripts are now known to us. Of more recent origin were the strange characters called *Runes,* which date back to the seventh and ninth centuries.

Runes were mainly used for carving inscriptions on stone monuments, of which about 4,000 remain in existence, while others were engraved upon coins, jewellery, crosses and swords. Runes are found in various parts of Britain, Scandinavia, Germany, France and Spain, and were most likely an early form of secret writing, based on an alphabet of 24 rather spindly-looking letters.

Runes were used by the Germanic peoples, who considered them to possess magic powers, but with the coming of Christianity, their use was discouraged, and their meaning was lost until archaeologists rediscovered it.

Oghams

Another ancient secret system of writing is called Oghams, used by the early Celtic peoples in Ireland, Scotland, and Wales. Oghams were, in fact, a kind of cipher, and examples can still be seen, mainly on very early tombstones. The system was based on a straight line, with other straight lines cut or inscribed across it. The Ogham alphabet had only 20 letters.

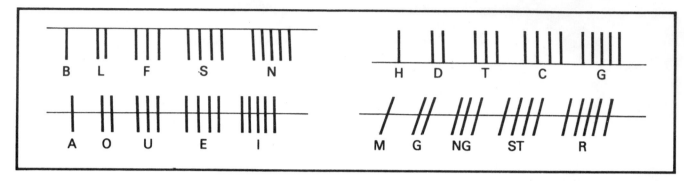

Even after Oghams had ceased to be used by the Celts, some people went on using them for secret messages, and this went on far into the Middle Ages. A book called *The Book of Ballymote*, published in Ireland in the 15th century, explained how to use Oghams for this purpose. Indeed, it is said that Charles I used Oghams for secret correspondence with Irish chieftains.

Charles I

12

It is still possible to make a cipher using Ogham characters, but in order to make it work, using the extra letters of the modern alphabet, a few more characters need to be added. Here is an example of one way of doing this:

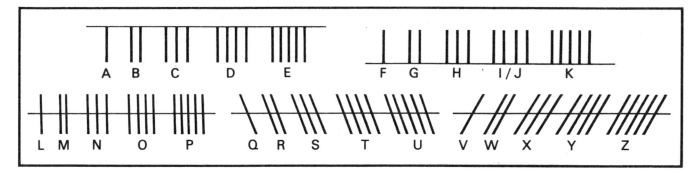

Using this modern adaptation of the old Ogham alphabet, here is a cipher message:

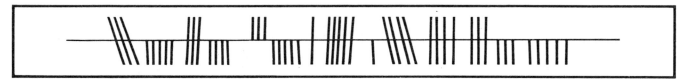

Can you read it? The answer is on page 72.

You can also adapt the Ogham alphabet for outdoor use, employing sticks and stones to form the characters, based on the following alphabet:

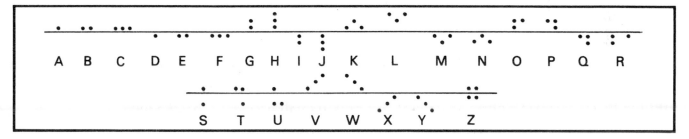

If you wished to leave a secret message for a friend (who must, of course, know the secret), you could work out something like this, using any convenient sticks and stones:

The deciphered message appears on page 72.

The idea of sending secret messages is a very old one, and all sorts of methods have been used. For convenience, the methods can be divided into three main groups: Concealment, in which a message is hidden or disguised, and Codes and Ciphers.

Codes

Codes and ciphers are two quite different things, although most people think of them as being the same. Codes, as we know, are not necessarily secret, while ciphers almost always are.

A code is simply a way of saying something by substituting different words, figures or symbols, often quite at random, but classifying them so that they can be recognised again. Any two people can devise their own code using two copies of an ordinary dictionary.

If you want to send the code word 'bird' to your partner, your dictionary may show the word on page 54, column one, line 16, so 'bird' appears encoded as 54:1:16, giving the page, column and line. All your partner has to do is look up page 54 in his dictionary, turn to column one, line 16, and of course, he will find the word 'bird'.

It is absolutely necessary for each person to use exactly the same edition of the dictionary. In fact, this is one of the weaknesses of codes generally. All codes need a kind of dictionary, or code-book, in which all the words or phrases used are listed with their meanings shown opposite. Foreign ambassadors nearly always use codes to send messages to their home countries.

Let us suppose that the following message was received by the British Ambassador in Belgrade:

SWORDFISH ARCTIC BELLFORT AFT CURRENT
MIDSHIPS WALRUS BOWSPRIT DOLPHIN

It is recognised as a code message, so the Ambassador's code expert would look up the message in the latest secret code-book, which might look like this:

AFT:	P.M.	BOWSPRIT:	MEET PLANE
ANCHOR:	DISPATCH NOW	CURRENT:	TOMORROW
ARCTIC:	ARRIVES BY AIR	DOLPHIN:	ARRANGE RECEPTION
BELLADONNA:	ONE	FORE:	A.M.
BELLDAME:	TWO	MERMAID:	QUEEN
BELLFORT:	THREE	MIDSHIPS:	CARRYING
BELLINGHAM:	FOUR	PACIFIC:	CANCEL INSTRUCTIONS
BELLKING:	FIVE	RIVER:	TODAY
BELLO:	ZERO	SPRAY:	LEAVING BY TRAIN
BELLPUSH:	SIX	SWORDFISH:	FOREIGN SECRETARY
BELLRING:	SEVEN	WALRUS:	SPECIAL ORDERS
BELLROCK:	EIGHT	WHALE:	PRIME MINISTER
BELLTIME:	NINE		

Such a message would quickly be decoded, and found to read:
FOREIGN SECRETARY ARRIVES BY AIR THREE P.M.
TOMORROW CARRYING SPECIAL ORDERS
MEET PLANE ARRANGE RECEPTION

The code-book, therefore, is essential to the understanding of the message. To cover every possible word or group of words, such code-books have to be very large, fat volumes, and must be kept in a very safe place. This can be dangerous, for the books can be stolen or copied, so the code has to be changed from time to time to make sure that secrets remain safe.

Zeppelin

Code-books carried on ships of most navies are usually bound in lead, so that if the books have to be destroyed quickly, they can be thrown overboard, when they will sink straight to the bottom of the ocean.

Yet sometimes, the commander of a vessel is unable to sink his code-books in time, and this is when the enemy can learn vital secrets.

Zeppelin Raids

During the First World War, the Germans made a number of air raids over Britain in huge Zeppelin airships. In October, 1917, the returning Zeppelins ran into a heavy storm. For some time, the big airships were tossed and thrown about in the gale, and the engineers used extra power to try to escape.

Soon, they had used up almost all of their fuel, giving them no choice but to make for the nearest coast and a forced landing. They were miles from Germany and the commanders quickly realised that the crews would almost certainly be captured if they survived. With little fuel left, two of the craft drifted over France. One disappeared from sight, but the other came to rest in a field near the headquarters of the U.S. Army. Soon, a number of American officers arrived on the scene to arrest the crew of the German airship. Among the Americans were several intelligence men, who were keen to discover the Zeppelin's code and cipher books, which they thought might still be on board.

Like other nations, the Germans usually kept their code-books in leaden boxes, but this was not possible on an airship, where weight carried had to be kept to the minimum. The books could not be burned either, since the gas used for lifting the airship was hydrogen, a highly explosive and dangerous element.

The airship was searched from stem to stern, but nothing was found. The Americans decided that the German crew would not have thrown the books overboard until they were certain of being captured. Working on this theory, Colonel Richard Williams, one of the intelligence men, decided to check back along the route.

Williams soon found some scraps of paper, and ordered his men to pick up every piece. Before long, the 'scraps' had been crammed into a number of large sacks. Everything was taken to headquarters, where dozens of men tried vainly to fit all the scraps together. While they were working, another officer, Lieutenant Hubbard, came into the room. Hubbard, a keen yachtsman, noticed that some of the scraps were blue in colour, and that the pieces were part of a naval chart.

With Hubbard's help, the chart was pieced together, and was discovered to be a complete guide to all the U-boats in the North Sea and English Channel, giving the code call-signs, and giving their positions. Another item found was a book giving a picture of all the ships and submarines in the German Navy, together with their call-signs and codes. The Allies were then able to destroy many of the German ships and all because the Germans had not been able to destroy their code-books in time.

Pasigraphy

Another form of code-system is called Pasigraphy, but this is not intended to be used for secrecy, but rather as a means of international communication. It is not used very much today, although a few such systems have been invented in recent years.

In 1852, a German named Anton Bachmaier published a book explaining his system, and giving a long list of words which had numbers as equivalents. The idea was to write a message, using his system of numbers, that anyone who had the right Pasigraphical dictionary in their own language could understand. For instance:

SEND ME TEN BOXES OF KNIVES AND FORKS

The word 'send' in Bachmaier's dictionary is given the number 2505; 'me' is 1605, 'ten' is 10, 'boxes' is 1241 (underlined to show plural), 1998 is 'knives', 3005 is 'and', while 1170 is 'forks'. So the complete message would be written: 2505 1605 10 1241 1998 3005 1170.

The fact that no one today has even heard of Anton Bachmaier or his idea indicates how successful was his system of Pasigraphy. Yet not long ago another German named André Eckhardt produced another system called 'Safo' which used special signs to convey meanings. Safo has 180 ideograms or signs, which can be put together to form meanings. For instance, Ⅎ means 'female', ꓶ means 'male', and Ⴘ means 'a parent'. Therefore, ⅎႸ means 'mother', ꓶႸ means 'father' and ꓶႸⅎ means 'parents'. The sign + before another symbol means 'small', and after a symbol means 'large'. A building is shown as ⬀, so +⬀ means 'a hut', while ⬀+ means 'a large house or palace'.

Many years ago, Lord Baden-Powell, founder of the Boy Scout movement, invented a system of signal-signs – 900 in all – for use by Scouts in sending messages over long distances. It is sometimes called the Scout language, but it cannot be spoken, only used for signalling. In fact, it is a kind of code.

International Languages

Naturally, the idea of using international codes for communication led people to the idea of an international spoken language, which is really a sort of code. The first idea of this sort which had any sort of success was called *Volapük*, invented by a German priest called Johann Martin Schleyer. But it was rather a complicated system and looked very strange when written down.

There have been several hundred other systems intended as international languages, but only one can boast any success. This is called Esperanto, and was invented by a Polish eye specialist called Ludovic Zamenhof. Zamenhof worked out his language so carefully that the entire rules of grammar can be printed on a single page of an ordinary-sized book. Esperanto is easy to learn, too, so many people still use it for international communication, either by writing or speaking.

In Esperanto, all nouns end in o, all adjectives end in a, adverbs in e, and infinitives of verbs in i. Zamenhof chose root-words from European languages; so that in Esperanto 'table' is *tablo,* 'dog' is *hundo,* 'cat' is *kato,* 'street' is *strato,* and so on. 'The dog is in the street' becomes *la hundo estas en la strato* in Esperanto.

Esperanto can really be regarded as a kind of code, too, because it is possible to buy a little book called an Esperanto 'key', which costs only a few pence. An Esperantist could write a letter or message to someone not knowing the language providing he enclosed the correct 'key' booklet, according to the language spoken by the recipient of the message.

Unusual Alphabets

In the Middle Ages, the vast majority of the people living were unable to read or write, so that important documents could only be read by the educated few. Because of this, kings, generals, ambassadors and so on, could be fairly sure that they could entrust messages to servants without that servant being able to pass on the information it contained. Such messages still fell into the wrong hands, and it was for this

John Brown's postcard

reason that ciphers and codes were employed. Yet even today, it is possible to disguise a message simply by putting it into an unknown language or even alphabet.

Take the case of John Brown, a German spy in Britain during the last War. Faced with the problem of loss of his code-books, he had to make contact with an agent, who was secretly serving aboard a Russian merchant-ship. Brown cleverly disguised his message, which looked something like the postcard illustrated on page 17.

However, as the postcard was passing through the Post Office, an alert security man noticed something rather odd about the card. The message looked like Russian, but the security man knew that the language was something else, although the writing was undoubtedly in Russian characters. First, he jotted down the longhand message in Russian 'printed' characters.

Next, he gave all the letters their nearest phonetic sounds in English, with the result that the message now read,

> *Dir Boris,*
> *Ai khav not bin ebl tu get ze matirial yu*
> *uonted, and aur kod-buks khav bin destroid bai*
> *fair. Kontakt mi az sun as posibl.*
> *Zh. Braun.*

Of course, the Russian sounds do not match English ones exactly, but it did not take the security man long to realise what the message said.

Mr. Brown soon received a reply to his postcard, but it was not the reply he expected!

Passports

Another early way of conveying secret information was by means of passports. These were invented in France during the reign of Louis XIV, who lived from 1638 to 1715. King Louis's Foreign Minister, the Count de Vergennes, suggested them as a kind of letter of introduction for foreign ambassadors when they came to France. The passports were provided by the French ambassadors in the various countries, and the foreign ambassadors were very pleased to have them, for they certainly made travelling about France easier.

However, the ambassadors would not have been so pleased had they realised that the 'passports' were really a secret way of checking the whereabouts of the ambassadors, and also for telling their backgrounds to the French king. In fact, much of the life history of each ambassador was contained in the passport, but concealed in a very ingenious way.

First of all, the passports were coloured according to the home country of the ambassador. If the man was English, the card was coloured yellow, the representative of Spain had a red passport, while green was shown on a Dutch passport. Portugal's was white, the one for Venice was white and yellow, red and green for Switzerland, green and yellow for Sweden, and green and white for Russia.

Even the age of the bearer could be told from the card, since an octagonal passport was issued to persons between 30 and 45, an oval one to those between 25 and 30, and a circular one to persons under 25.

Special lines under the man's name gave his description: wavy parallel lines meant he was tall and thin, while other variations of the lines showed he was tall, fat or short. Flowered ornaments were used

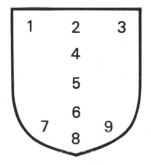

Points of the shield

1. Dexter chief
2. Middle chief
3. Sinister chief
4. Honour point
5. Fesse point
6. Nombril point
7. Dexter base
8. Middle point
9. Sinister base

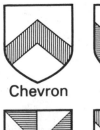

Chevron Bend

Gyronny Saltire

to show whether the ambassador was friendly and open, morose, thoughtful or otherwise.

Around the top of the card was a ribbon, which, by its length, indicated that the bearer was married, single or a widower, and another kind of ornament showed whether he was rich or poor. Full-stops, commas and semi-colons after the man's name gave his religion — a stop for a Catholic, a comma for a Protestant, a semi-colon for a Lutheran, or a dash if the man was Jewish.

By these means, a member of King Louis's court could tell, by looking at the ambassador's passport, whether the visitor was to be trusted or not, even what his skills and occupation might be. The whole thing was an elaborate type of code.

Heraldry

An ancient science which uses a peculiar system of codes all its own is heraldry. There is nothing secret in the system, of course, although the descriptive words used are often mystifying to people who know nothing about heraldry. These words are derived from Old French, although they are pronounced in the English way. *Gules*, for instance, simply means red, while *Azure* is blue, *Vert* is green, *Purpure* is purple, *Sable*, black, *Tenne*, orange, *Sanguine*, dark red, *Or*, gold, and *Argent*, silver or white.

The main part of a coat of arms is the shield, which is known in heraldry as an Escutcheon, and the various parts of the Escutcheon also have names, as shown in the picture. 'Dexter' means left, as you look at the shield, and 'Sinister' means right.

Escutcheons are ornamented by 'metals', 'colours', and 'furs', all of which have their own special names, and the Escutcheon itself is usually divided up into several parts. The lines used for the divisions may be wavy, zigzag, or may take some other form, each of which has its own descriptive title.

The shield, or Escutcheon of the Royal Arms, for instance, is divided into four quarters, numbered from one to four. To describe it, heraldic experts say that the Escutcheon is 'Quarterly 1st and 4th England (that is, the Arms of England appear on the 1st and 4th quarters), 2nd Scotland and 3rd Ireland. This means that the Arms of Scotland appear in the 2nd quarter, and those of Ireland in the 3rd. The supporters of the Royal Arms are 'On the dexter side (left), a lion guardant, crowned or (meaning a lion standing and looking out from the shield, and wearing a golden crown); on the sinister (right), a unicorn argent maned and unguled or, gorged and chained of the same (meaning a silver unicorn with golden mane and hooves, and with golden collar and chain).

All this information is shown on the Arms by the code system of heraldry, which is also international, at least so far as the old states of Europe are concerned. The rules which apply to heraldry have also been used on flags, and in fact, the Royal Standard flag is simply the four quarters of the shield placed on a flag.

Flags, of course, are also used in signalling, for which an entirely new system was invented by Rear-Admiral Richard Kempenfelt in the latter part of the 18th century. The system was used by the Royal Navy, but it has been revised over the years, and the whole code has now been adopted internationally.

Signalling

Just before the Battle of Trafalgar, on 21st October, 1805, a line of coloured flags appeared above the flagship *Victory*. The captains of the other ships in the fleet were able to read a message which spelled out the words 'England expects that every man will do his duty'.

This is probably the most famous message for which Naval signalling flags were used, and although the coloured signal flags are still employed today, they are now less important than such systems as radio, semaphore, Morse, and others.

The International Code of Signals at sea uses 40 different flags, 26 of them are alphabetical, representing each letter of the Latin alphabet. Ten are numerical, covering the digits 1 to zero, and the others are special signalling flags.

Messages sent by these flags are flown from a halyard, and they are read from the top of the halyard downwards. A signal halyard usually sends a complete message at one time, although large ships can sometimes hoist a number of halyards, each with a different signal.

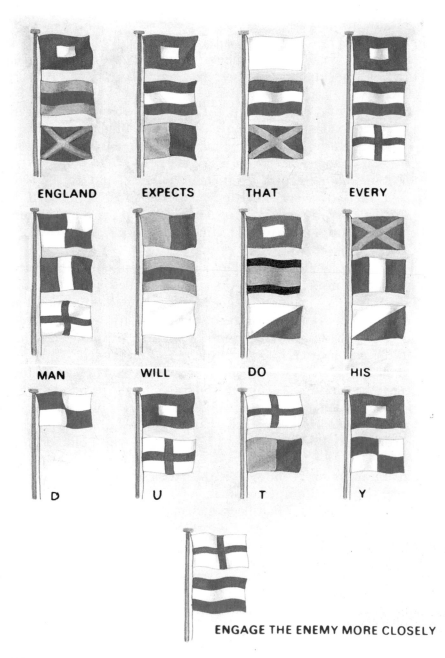

ENGLAND   EXPECTS   THAT   EVERY

MAN   WILL   DO   HIS

D   U   T   Y

ENGAGE THE ENEMY MORE CLOSELY

Flagship *Victory*

Obviously, if messages were all sent alphabetically, the same number of flags as letters would be required, so usually the numeral pendants are used to send code numbers. These numbers are all contained in a General Signal Book, a large volume in which hundreds of useful phrases are classified. The number 287 might mean 'proceed at once', and would be signalled on the halyard with the three numerical pendants for 2, 8 and 7 instead of 13 alphabetical flags.

The alphabetical flags are also used in code combinations, and these are contained in the Vocabulary Signal Book. These flags are used largely for more general communication, with the numerical pendants signalling orders. NC, for instance, means 'I am in distress and require immediate assistance'. For convenience and brevity, therefore, messages are always sent in code, and the only time that the flags are used to spell out words is when an unusual one, such as a name, needs to be sent.

The best known of all signalling codes is probably the Morse Code, which strictly speaking is not a code at all, but a cipher. However, since it is used for communications, it is more convenient to think of it as a code. Since it is easy to learn, the Morse code ought to be mastered by everyone, even if only for fun.

Samuel Morse invented the electric telegraph, but in order to make the apparatus work, it needed some system of ordered sounds, so he invented the Morse Code, which, as everyone knows, is a system of 'dots and dashes'.

Morse can be sent in many different ways: by an electric buzzer, by flashes on a lamp or torch, or by using a mirror to reflect sunlight. It can even be tapped out in beats upon a wall or floor or other sounding board. Any lamp can be used for sending Morse, even an oil one, since all that is necessary is to cover the lamp to break the message into long and short flashes. Any system using sound can be employed for Morse sending – even blasts on a siren or whistle.

The Morse Code was first heard in 1837, but this was not the first method of sending signals over long distances. One of the earliest was the 'telegraphic machine' invented by Aeneas Tacticus in 350 B.C. His method was to fill a small pot with water, with some means for drawing off, or adding to the water inside. A notched stick fixed to a cork was floated on the surface of the water, and a flaming torch was lit at the top of the stick. This apparatus could be seen for some miles, and codes were devised according to how high or low the stick was standing in the water. The notches on the stick measured the distance travelled by the stick. During times of war, a stick standing at a certain height might mean 'send reinforcements', or 'city taken by invaders'.

About one hundred years later, the Greek historian Polybius worked out a better system, using ten torches to indicate individual letters, so that complete messages could be sent.

Amazingly complicated messages, using sound only, can be sent by Africans using native drums. These drums are made from hollowed-out logs, and beaten by small wooden mallets. Messages are sent by a code system something like Morse, but which uses not only 'long' and 'short' sounds, but also high and low tones. African drummers send their messages at a very fast rate, and large drums can be heard as much as twenty miles away. One drum message can be

picked up by another operator, and the message can be then relayed to yet another, so that news can be broadcast very quickly.

A similar system was used by the Romans when they built Hadrian's Wall. Inside the wall, the Romans placed long, hollow pipes which were used for communication from one sentry post to the next. Using a system rather like Morse, messages were sent by tapping on the pipes, which carried the sound along to the next post. It was also possible to send messages by word of mouth simply by shouting into the pipe, although it is doubtful if even the Romans believed what a later writer thought possible. That is, that if you shouted into a hollow pipe, and then quickly corked it up, the sound would be retained inside, and come rolling out when the cork was pulled!

African drummers

Signals and Sign Language

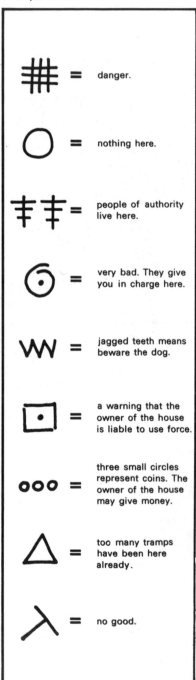

= danger.

○ = nothing here.

≠ ≢ = people of authority live here.

ⓖ = very bad. They give you in charge here.

ᗯᗯ = jagged teeth means beware the dog.

▣ = a warning that the owner of the house is liable to use force.

○○○ = three small circles represent coins. The owner of the house may give money.

△ = too many tramps have been here already.

⅄ = no good.

In the days when much international trade and business was carried out in China, many Europeans had offices, factories and shipping businesses in the large cities, employing many Chinese people. The Chinese are by nature very polite and appreciate politeness in others, as they also appreciate good treatment on the part of employers. Some of the more overbearing European employers were somewhat mystified when their businesses failed to prosper as well as those of other Europeans.

The reason, in fact, was quite simple. The Chinese, although speaking a number of different dialects which are not mutually understood, have a common system of writing. A man from Canton, for instance, writes in Chinese ideograms in exactly the same way as a man, say, from Pekin, although they speak different tongues. The Chinese had also developed a system of secret marks, which could be placed on the outside of a man's house, on his goods, motor cars, and even on his personal baggage. Therefore, when a 'bad' employer despatched goods, travelled by car, train, or other means, the secret mark appeared somewhere, telling all Chinese that the man was unworthy. Because of this, he found porters handled his goods badly, his servants would not stay long at his house, and his business failed to prosper because of delays, accidents, and other causes. A good employer, on the other hand, would find willing helpers wherever he went, and so became very successful in all his dealings in China.

The Chinese people are not confined to China itself, but are found in many parts of Asia and the Pacific. Yet the secret signs are understood by every Chinese wherever he may be, so that success or failure would follow a businessman wherever he went. The Chinese code of markings probably helped many men to succeed in life, but it probably sent many others into bankruptcy.

Tramps' and Gypsies' Codes

In Europe, a system of secret signs has been developed by tramps. This code is, of course, used for passing on information to each other, but the uncanny thing is that for quite a long while, no one knew that such a thing existed. One day, however, the French police arrested a tramp on a minor charge, and found a scrap of paper in his pocket which gave the information about the tramps' code. The signs shown are usually marked on the wall of a house by one tramp, so that when another one comes along, he will know what to expect from the people in that home.

A very similar code is used by the Gypsies. In fact, it is possible that the tramps copied the code idea from the Gypsies. Apart from their code, the Gypsies have a language of their own as well as a strange alphabet, which differs according to whether it is used by men, elders of the tribe, or by children.

The Gypsy language is related to the languages of India, the original home of the Gypsies before they began roving across Asia and into Europe centuries ago. Some Gypsy words have made their way into English, such as 'romany' for Gypsy, and 'dad' for father. In addition to their secret code, or 'patrin', the Gypsies also use common objects in a private system of communication. Each tribe, for instance, has its own sign, or totem, such as a moon, sun, badger, pine tree, and so on. When a tribe leaves a camping ground, and moves on to another place, it often leaves a message for other Gypsies who might call.

Gypsy fortune-telling

The badger tribe might leave a hazel twig fixed to a tree, tied with a thread of cotton. Beneath it would be a rough carving of a badger's head. To a visiting Gypsy, the signs would mean that a child had been born to the badger tribe: a boy if a red thread was used, and a girl if the thread was white.

Gypsies, of course, are renowned for their fortune-telling, but some of their apparently amazing knowledge is quite simply explained. A Gypsy woman calling at a house in the country to sell clothes-pegs, wax flowers and other goods, will be very observant and will take the opportunity to find out something of the family in the house. When she leaves, the Gypsy will leave some information behind her, secretly marked in chalk in some not-too-obvious position. The marks, of course, will be in the Gypsy 'patrin' code, and will only be understood

25

by other gypsies. If another Gypsy should call at the house, she would then be able to 'astonish' the occupiers with her knowledge of them.

Stage 'Magic'

Another group of people who can perform what appear to be miraculous feats of thought-reading and telepathy, are, of course, stage magicians. As everyone knows, they are really using some system of code, which can be so cleverly thought out, that the audience cannot detect its use. The usual method is for the 'thought-reader' to be blind-folded, while the magician himself holds up objects to be identified.

A simple code for identifying the cards in a pack could be worked like this: the magician may be alone on the stage, but has a telephone on the table. A member of the audience picks out a card, the magician says he will speak to a person by telephone, who will read his thoughts. He dials a number, speaks, and the distant person's voice is heard over a loud speaker, telling the correct card chosen.

What happens is that the magician and his accomplices have worked out a code perhaps on the lines of the following:

HEARTS:	Heath; Hawkins; Hobbs	NINE:	Norman; Norma
CLUBS:	Cameron; Chandler; Clark	EIGHT:	Eric; Eileen
DIAMONDS:	Davis; Dunn; Dyer	SEVEN:	Sydney; Sheila
SPADES:	Spalding; Stevens; Strong	SIX:	Stephen; Stella
ACE:	Arthur; Alice	FIVE:	Frank; Frances
KING:	Kenneth; Kathleen	FOUR:	Philip; Phyllis
QUEEN:	Brian; Betty	THREE:	Thomas; Thelma
JACK:	John; Joan	TWO:	Talbot; Trudy
TEN:	Timothy; Tanya		

The chosen card is the Queen of Hearts. Each of the magician's accomplices is sitting by his telephone with a copy of the code. The magician simply dials one of the numbers, and asks for Mr. Brian Heath (or Hawkins, or Hobbs). If the accomplice is a woman, then he will ask for Miss (or Mrs.) Betty Heath (or Hawkins or Hobbs). The accomplice then refers to his code, and knows that the chosen card was the Queen of Hearts, and announces this over the phone.

Thought-Reading

Codes can be used for all kinds of thought-reading, and a popular party game uses a simple one of this kind. An object is chosen while the thought-reader is out of the room. When he returns, the operator points to various objects and when he points to the chosen object, the thought-reader is able to identify it correctly. Of course, the code is worked by pointing first to a prearranged object, such as something beginning with a particular letter of the alphabet.

The code can be sometimes made more complicated by arranging for the operator to casually hold out a number of fingers to indicate when the correct object will be shown. Thus, five fingers will mean that the fifth object is correct, four will indicate that it will be the fourth, and so on.

All these systems are very simple, and it would not be long before the audience spotted the secret. However, professional magicians use very complicated codes. For instance, in choosing cards, the magician can signal meanings by various secret means. If asked a question by the assistant, the magician can remain silent. This can indicate a particular card, as can the simple answers 'Yes' or 'No', 'Of course', 'Correct', or 'Good'. A red card could be indicated if the magician remained silent, while if he said 'Yes' or 'No', the assistant would know that this meant a black card. The same sort of operation would show which of the two suits was then correct. The rest of the code could be worked out as shown on the right.

The chosen card is the Nine of Spades. The assistant, who does not know the chosen card, will begin: "Let me see, I believe you're thinking of a card." The magician would answer 'yes', indicating to his assistant that the chosen card was a black one, that is, either spades or clubs. "Ah," continues the assistant, "I'm pretty sure it's a black card!" The magician then stays quite silent, and this tells his assistant something more, for they had previously agreed that a silence meant a heart if the suit was red, or a spade if the suit was black. If the magician had replied 'yes' to the question, then the assistant would have known he meant either a club or a diamond.

"It's a spade!" says the assistant.

"Quite correct!" says the magician. From this, the assistant remembers the code, and recalls that 'quite correct' meant a nine.

"The card is the Nine of Spades!" ends the assistant, and is quite right, since the magician has, of course, 'told' him the answer by means of the code.

A code such as this can be adapted for use with other objects, such as coins, clothing, and room furnishings. The main requirement in these cases is for the magician and his assistant to have good memories, since the code, of course, has to be recalled with accuracy.

Another code connected with playing-cards is the system used by card-sharpers who employ specially marked cards. Such packs are made with a design on the back that allows the card-sharper to read the suits and values of each individual card. There are various ways that this can be done, and one design is shown on the right.

If you study the design of the circular device in the corner of the card, you will see that some of the small discs are coloured in, while others are white. In fact, it is the white discs which show the identity of the card. The discs, by their position, indicate which card is meant, King, Queen, Jack, 10, 9, and so on, while the disc in the very centre indicates an Ace. The 'flower' in the middle shows the suit, so that a 'petal' without a dark tone indicates which, from the sequence Hearts, Clubs, Diamonds, Spades, is intended.

Another system used for marking cards needs a special kind of fluorescent ink, or else a coloured ink which is not immediately obvious to the naked eye. The card-sharper wears a special kind of dark glasses, through which the identity of the cards can be read from the markings made in the special inks. Other card-sharpers use hand signals and signs to inform their accomplices of the cards they are holding.

Hand Signals
Hand signals, in fact, form an important branch of codes, both secret, and for general use. Traffic police use a system known to every motorist, but there are others used by Scouts, the Army and Navy, and by people responsible for guiding aircraft when they land.

ACE:	Yes
KING:	Correct
QUEEN:	Silent
JACK:	Of course
TEN:	Oh yes
NINE:	Quite Correct
EIGHT:	Right
SEVEN:	That's right
SIX:	True
FIVE:	Quite true
FOUR:	O.K.
THREE:	Yes, it is
TWO:	Uh–huh.

Four of Clubs

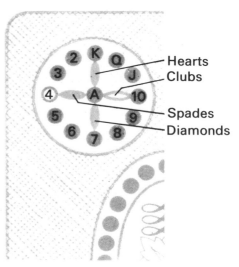

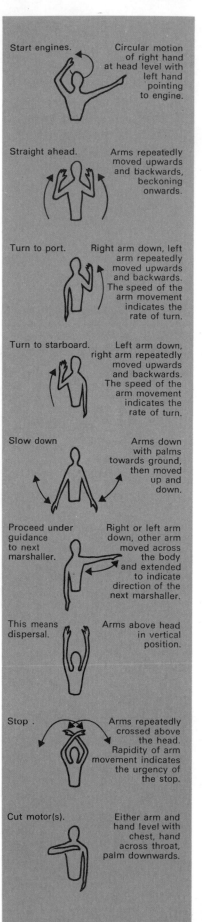

Start engines. Circular motion of right hand at head level with left hand pointing to engine.

Straight ahead. Arms repeatedly moved upwards and backwards, beckoning onwards.

Turn to port. Right arm down, left arm repeatedly moved upwards and backwards. The speed of the arm movement indicates the rate of turn.

Turn to starboard. Left arm down, right arm repeatedly moved upwards and backwards. The speed of the arm movement indicates the rate of turn.

Slow down Arms down with palms towards ground, then moved up and down.

Proceed under guidance to next marshaller. Right or left arm down, other arm moved across the body and extended to indicate direction of the next marshaller.

This means dispersal. Arms above head in vertical position.

Stop . Arms repeatedly crossed above the head. Rapidity of arm movement indicates the urgency of the stop.

Cut motor(s). Either arm and hand level with chest, hand across throat, palm downwards.

One of the ways used for international 'conversation' is sign language. We have all tried talking by making signs, particularly when in a foreign country. Signs are made on the spur of the moment and not surprisingly, are often misunderstood.

'Deaf' and 'Dumb' Alphabets

Yet not all sign language is so haphazard. As early as the 16th century, Pedro Ponce de Leon, a Spanish Benedictine monk, devised a code which helped to 'teach the deaf to speak, read, write, reckon, pray, serve at the altar, know Christian doctrine, and confess with a loud voice'. Whether all these claims were ever fulfilled is open to question, but Ponce de Leon did achieve much progress with his sign language, in a system which was later used by his pupil, Juan Pablo Bonet.

The first book on the subject in Britain was written by John Bulwer, and published in 1648, followed by another by George Dalgarno, a Scot, who published details of a two-handed deaf-and-dumb alphabet of signs. Nowadays there are two systems of hand alphabets used by the deaf. The two-handed alphabet is used largely in Great Britain, while the United States and most other countries use a one-handed alphabet. Both are shown below.

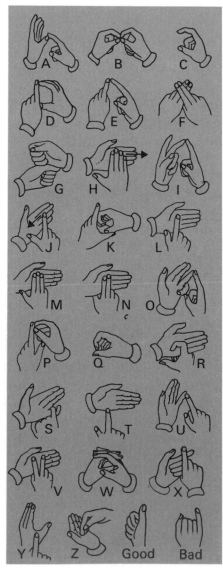

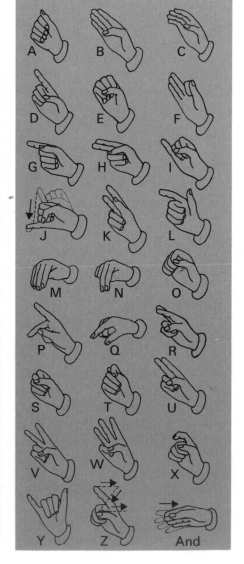

Indian Sign Language

Quite another system of sign language is used by the Plains Indians of North America. Despite the fact that there are over thirty different Indian tribes, each speaking a different tongue, they are able to talk in an intricate hand-language. The Indians themselves have used this sign-language for centuries, and as American civilisation moved to the West, so the pioneer travellers found it necessary to learn the Indians' code of signs.

Unlike the European deaf-and-dumb systems, which are alphabetic, the Indians' use of signs covers whole words and phrases. For instance, the palm of the hand held over the mouth means astonishment or surprise, while fondness is expressed by holding the hand over the heart.

More complicated ideas are expressed by combining simple signs. YOUR HOUSE IS ON FIRE would be expressed in sign language in the following manner:

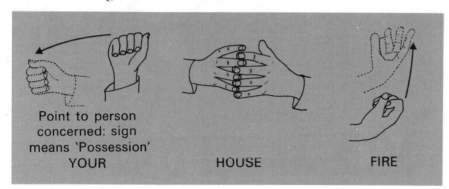

Here are more expressions:
WHITE MAN SPEAK WITH FORKED TONGUE
(i.e., tells a lie)

HAS THE WAGON TRAIN PASSED THIS WAY?

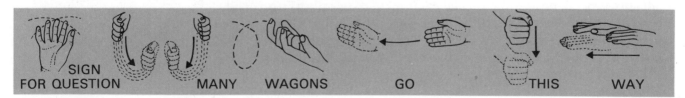

THEY WENT THAT WAY

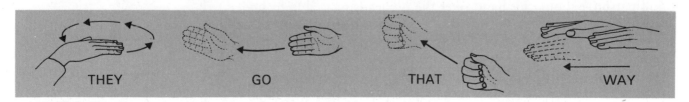

The other famous Indian method of communication was for sending messages over distances, using the smoke of fires. Smoke-signals have, of course, been used by other peoples, although more advanced ideas have since taken their place. From early times, men had stood on hill-tops signalling to their neighbours on another hill, usually by just waving their arms, which was how the semaphore alphabet came into being.

Semaphore

Obviously, semaphore can only be used during the daytime, and only on clear days, at that. The system uses a different position of the arms to indicate each letter, but in order to make it easier to see from a distance, flags are nearly always used. The colour and design of the flags do not matter, so long as they are easily seen.

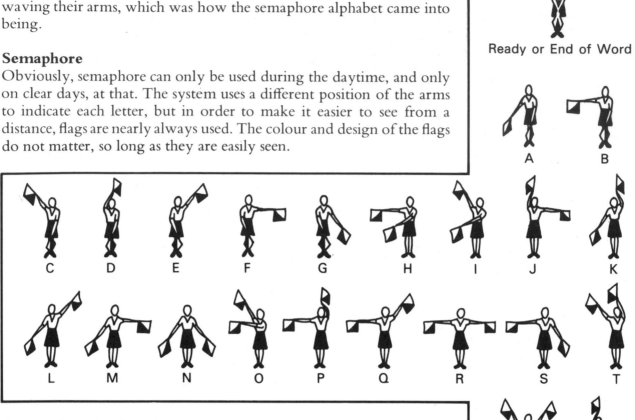

Semaphore Alphabet

As semaphore developed, more complicated apparatus was introduced, such as tall poles fitted with movable arms.

On sunny days, signallers learned to use the light of the sun to flash messages with polished pieces of metal or glass, in a system which came to be called the Heliograph. It is still in use, although the Morse alphabet is usually employed nowadays.

Reading Systems for the Blind

All these systems of communication depend, of course, on the receiver being able to see the signals. Blind people, naturally, cannot use them at all and, indeed, need some special equipment to be able to read at all. There have been dozens of ideas for helping the blind to read, but the real breakthrough came when a blind French boy grew up, remembering vaguely the joys of seeing. He had gone blind at the age of three in 1812, and for many years he had experimented with ways of reading and writing for the blind.

Success came when he worked out quite a simple plan. He stuck pins into a cushion, each group of pins representing a letter, and a blind person, rubbing his hand over the pinheads, was able to understand the message there. It was the beginning of the Braille system, for its inventor was the man who had gone blind at three years old, Louis Braille.

Braille's system, in fact a kind of cipher, using upraised dots instead of letters, looks like the sketch at the top of page 31.

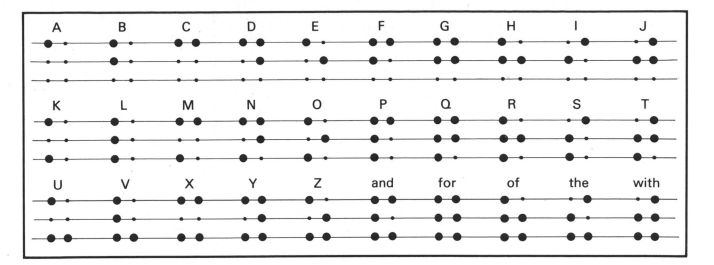

The upraised dots are punched into thick paper, which can then be bound like an ordinary book. The Braille alphabet contains not only alphabetical signs, but also symbols for the more common complete words, such as 'and', 'for', and 'of'. Another system was invented by Doctor William Moon, an Englishman, whose letters, like those of Braille, were embossed on paper or other surfaces. Moon's letters, however, were simplified versions of the ordinary Latin ones:

This alphabet is still in use, mainly by those who find the Braille dot system too difficult to master.

Shorthand

A very early system of secret writing was invented more than two thousand years ago by a former Roman slave named Tullius Tyro. This was a code of sorts consisting of a kind of shorthand called, after its inventor, Tyronian characters, or 'notes'. These characters were used for some time afterwards, and by the Middle Ages over 1,300 different signs were known.

Although Tullius Tyro is sometimes said to have invented shorthand, it was in all probability first used by the Greeks, who called it 'tachygraphy' or 'swift writing'. This was not intended to be secret, although it was based on a type of abbreviated writing used for secret communications among the early Christians.

Shorthand really began with a book published in 1588, in which its author, Doctor Timothy Bright, explained his new system. Although quite difficult compared with modern shorthand, Bright's system looked similar to those in use today. It is shown on page 32.

Bright's shorthand

Although there are several shorthand systems, the two most widely used are the Pitman and Gregg versions. Both are based on the **sounds** of words, rather than the spelling, and both use simple symbols or outlines to write the system on paper.

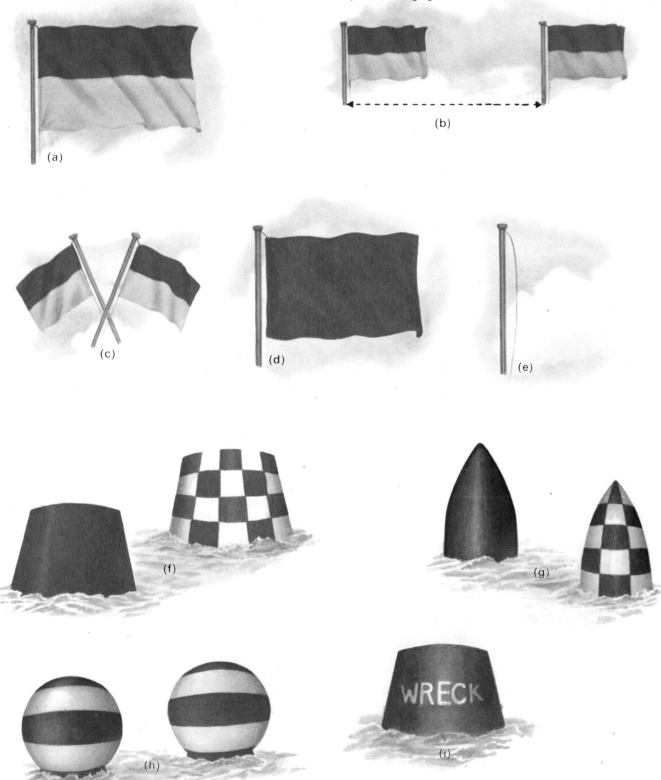

(a)

(b)

(c)

(d)

(e)

(f)

(g)

(h)

WRECK

(i)

Various sign systems
Aircraft signals
Special signs are placed on the ground for the information of pilots of aircraft when they fly over airfields. A forty-foot square, usually placed near the control area, is set aside for the use of these signs.

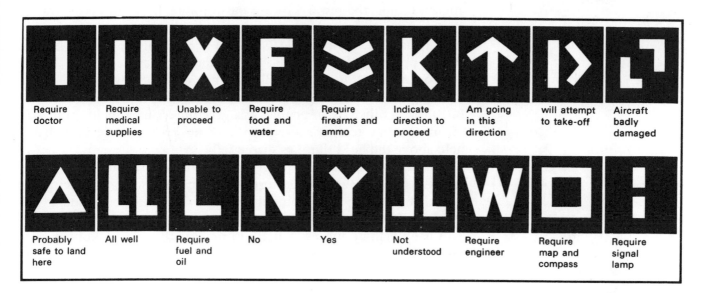

When pilots are forced down, they may find that their radio is damaged beyond repair, and need some means of communication with possible rescue planes. A proper International Ground-to-Air Emergency Code has been worked out for the use of crashed aircraft crews, which can be understood by all pilots, no matter what their language. The signs can be made by marks in the ground or sand, by using pieces of white material, or simply by arranging sticks in the agreed positions.

Above and right:
International Ground-to-Air Emergency Code

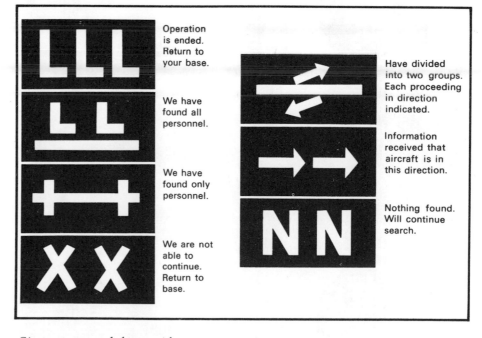

Left: Signs at sea and the seaside
(a) Area patrolled by lifeguards
(b) Safe bathing area between masts
(c) Unsafe to bathe
(d) Area not patrolled by lifeguards
(e) Safe bathing area
(f) Port hand buoys
(g) Starboard hand buoys
(h) Middle ground buoys
(i) Wreck buoy

Signs at sea and the seaside
If you spend any time by the sea, you will often see various flags on the beach which give information about the safety or otherwise of bathing. The flags will appear as shown in the picture on page 32.

Gestures

The gestures made with the hands when speaking make a kind of code which is almost international. For instance, to hold up the fist, thumb uppermost, is taken as a gesture of something good, but the fist held with the thumb downwards is assumed to mean something bad. Yet in ancient Rome, the gestures meant the opposite. If the Emperor, watching gladiators in combat in the arena, held his thumb upwards, it meant that the victor should go ahead and kill his opponent, but the thumb downwards meant that the life should be spared.

Crossing the fingers generally means good luck whilst the hands held together usually signify prayer, but the same gesture is used by Indians and other Asian peoples as a greeting. A hand held up in class means that the teacher's attention is being called, while both hands held above the head signifies surrender.

Raising the hat is almost universal in Europe, as a salute or greeting. It comes from the ancient gesture of raising the visor on the helmet of a suit of armour; a movement which would only be made in the presence of a friend.

A hand held up means 'halt' almost everywhere; a beckoning hand means 'come here'; a handshake is taken as a sign of friendship anywhere in the world and waving is a popular form of saying farewell.

Gladiators in combat

Ciphers

Five hundred years before the birth of Christ, a Greek named Histiaeus was serving at the court of Persia. He wished to send a secret message to his son-in-law, who was at home in Greece. It was important that no one should discover the message, for it urged Histiaeus's son-in-law, Aristagorus, to begin a rebellion against the rulers of the state. Histiaeus had a bright idea. He sent for his slave and took him into a closed room. Some time later, the slave emerged and sped on his way.

Months later spies from the Greek government eventually stopped the slave on his journey, and threw him into prison. They suspected that he carried a secret message and after a thorough search, they ripped open the slave's sandal, and discovered a folded papyrus.

Highly pleased with their work, the spies took the papyrus to the ruler of the state, who, when he read the message, was convinced he knew the secrets of Histiaeus. So sure was he, that when later the slave managed to escape, the king did not even bother to have him followed. Shortly afterwards, the slave reached Aristagorus, and gave him the verbal message, 'Shave my head and look thereon!' Aristagorus had the slave's head shaved, anh there, tattooed upon the now bald pate, was a message from Histiaeus, telling him to begin the rebellion. The other papyrus found by the spies was a dummy, deliberately placed so as to throw the enemy off the scent.

All through the ages, people have tried to hide messages in this way. Codes, which we have already examined, were used from early times, and so were various methods of *hiding* the message.

Of course, not all messages were sent by spies and agents. Some were sent by ordinary people who wanted to keep their message a secret, or to dodge payment in some way. For instance, in the days before the introduction to Great Britain of the Penny Post by Rowland Hill in 1840, the charge for carrying letters was very high indeed, and plenty of people avoided using the post if they possibly could, getting travelling friends to carry letters for them.

A newspaper was the only article which could be sent through the post without charge. The reason was that the government had already put a heavy tax on newspapers and had decided that they could not tax such an article again. Many people tried to send letters by hiding them inside the newspapers, but the penalties for doing such a thing were severe, and the culprits were nearly always discovered. This did not deter the public from trying, as a letter in those days cost about one shilling for every hundred miles, and a shilling in those days was worth a great deal.

Soon, however, people worked out a clever trick. Instead of putting a written note inside the newspapers, the senders made tiny marks or pinpricks over the tops of certain letters on the printed page. The letters, when spelled out in sequence, formed a message. This was a form of cipher, and one which was rarely discovered at the time.

A cipher, unlike a code, needed no books to decipher it, and most of the best ones could be carried without recourse to anything but the memory. Apart from the expedient of hiding a message, there are two main types of cipher: the transposition cipher, and the substitution cipher. This is not as complicated as it sounds. A transposition cipher simply means that the actual letters of the message are jumbled up in such a way that only the person who knows the secret can re-arrange the letters in the correct order, and so read the message.

Transposition Ciphers

Most schoolchildren have tried their hands at simple transposition ciphers. For instance, REWOT DENIUR DLO EHT TA EM TEEM would not fool anyone for long. It is a sentence in English spelled backwards, and when read properly says, MEET ME AT THE OLD RUINED TOWER. Very few spies would be foolish enough to try that one!

Messages can be hidden within other words or phrases, and a simple example of this is the *acrostic*. At first glance, the list of words on the right means nothing.

TIME
HILL
EXTENDED
COWARD
ASSISI
TARIFF
AVENUE
NORTH
DIRECT

But if you read the initial letters only, down the column of words, a phrase will appear; and reading the final letters of each word upwards from the bottom will complete the phrase.

Even a slight rearrangement of the letters of a sentence will make it much more difficult to read. THE QUICK BROWN FOX JUMPS OVER THE LAZY DOG makes difficult reading if all the words are run together. THEQUICKBROWNFOXJUMPSOVERTHE LAZYDOG. But if the letters are arranged in a block, it is harder still to read.

T	H	E	Q	U	I	C
K	B	R	O	W	N	F
O	X	J	U	M	P	S
O	V	E	R	T	H	E
L	A	Z	Y	D	O	G

More difficult still would be to decipher the sentence when written with each alternate line reversed.

T	H	E	Q	U	I	C
F	N	W	O	R	B	K
O	X	J	U	M	P	S
E	H	T	R	E	V	O
L	A	Z	Y	D	O	G

The message could also be written in columns that read upwards, and each of the horizontal lines then rewritten in sequence: CFSEG INPHO UWMTD QOURY ERJEZ HBXVA TKOOL. The sentence is now quite difficult to decipher. However, a skilled cryptographer, that is, someone expert in codes and ciphers, could work out the answer to this one in a few minutes, without knowing the secret beforehand.

C	F	S	E	G
I	N	P	H	O
U	W	M	T	D
Q	O	U	R	Y
E	R	J	E	Z
H	B	X	V	A
T	K	O	O	L

A much better type of transposition cipher is one using a keyword. A keyword is chosen containing six or seven letters, each of which must be different. Using the word DELIGHT as the keyword, this word is first written down and under it, in regular columns. Ignoring the spaces between words, the message MEET ME AT THE OLD RUINED TOWER is written as before. As the message does not quite fill up the block, three 'dummy' letters A, B and C have been added. These dummy letters are called 'nulls'.

D	E	L	I	G	H	T
M	E	E	T	M	E	A
T	T	H	E	O	L	D
R	U	I	N	E	D	T
O	W	E	R	A	B	C

The next stage is to write above the keyword, figures which show the order of the letters in DELIGHT as they occur in the alphabet.

1	2	6	5	3	4	7
D	E	L	I	G	H	T

The letters of the keyword, and also the letters appearing in each of the columns below, should now be arranged in the correct *numerical* order.

1	2	3	4	5	6	7
D	E	G	H	I	L	T
M	E	M	E	T	E	A
T	T	O	L	E	H	D
R	U	E	D	N	I	T
O	W	A	B	R	E	C

37

Then, the letters can be written in a line of seven-letter groups:

MEMETEA TTOLEHD RUEDNIT OWABREC

This makes a very mysterious-looking cipher message. But the person receiving the message will know the keyword and will be able to decipher the message by writing out the message in columns, as it appears in the block above, and then placing the keyword (with the letters in the numerical order DEGHILT) above it. By writing in the block again, but this time, putting the columns in the correct order of the word DELIGHT, the message can now be read as it was originally written.

A simpler transposition cipher is called the 'Railfence' cipher, because it is written in a zigzag fashion, rather like the top of a fence. Using the same message MEET ME AT THE OLD RUINED TOWER, this would be written out in the Railfence cipher as:

M E M A T E L R I E T W R
  E T E T H O D U N D O E

The first letter of the message is written in the top line, the second letter in the bottom line, the third in the top line, and so on. Then the message is written out as it appears in the rows:

MEMATELRIETWR ETETHODUNDOE

As the message now looks rather clumsy, it is then divided into five-letter groups, MEMAT ELRIE TWRET ETHOD UNDOE.

When deciphering the railfence cipher it is important to write the message out in two rows, one above the other, always starting with the first letter on the top row.

The Scytale
One of the earliest ways of jumbling up words in this way was by using a *scytale* (pronounced "see-tah'ly" or "skee-tah'ly"). Scytales were used by the ancient Greeks, Romans, Egyptians and others for sending secret messages. The most important items of equipment were two wooden staffs, which had to be of exactly the same circumference.

A long, continuous narrow strip of parchment or papyrus was wrapped around the staff like a bandage, arranged in such a way that the bandage spread along the staff in a corkscrew pattern. The message was carefully written along the wound-on bandage, so that each letter appeared on one of the turns. The parchment was then unwound, and re-rolled into a compact spool, which the messenger hid away.

Sometimes, if the message-senders wanted to be extra clever, they would actually use a bandage, worn by the carrier on his arm or leg to cover an apparent wound. Once the messenger reached his destination safely, all that remained was to wind the parchment strip (or bandage) on to another, identical staff, when the message could be read easily.

It is still possible to use this method of sending messages today by using a broom-handle or even a pencil, wound with a strip of paper, but the recipient of the message must have a broom-handle or pencil just like the sender's.

A scytale, used in Ancient Greece to send secret messages.

Concealment Ciphers

Cipher messages can also be hidden in the body of another message in such a way that only the possessor of the secret is able to read the hidden message. It can be done by using a grille like the one shown on the right.

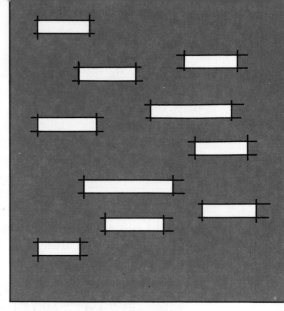

The secret message is written through the holes in the grille. This is then removed, and the sender writes in a dummy letter to disguise the secret message. On the right is a letter written in this way.

The words composing the secret message have been shaded in, and read: WANTED AT ONCE COMPLETE INFORMATION REGARDING SHIPPING NOW OPERATING FROM ALL CENTRAL AREAS. Spies become very skilled in using gadgets such as the grille, but one British spy—whom we shall call Thomas Helliwell—met his end through not being clever enough to detect a cipher message when he saw one.

Thomas Helliwell was really a double agent, which means he was spying for both Britain and an enemy power. Helliwell was selling all sorts of secrets to both sides, and was under the impression that his double-dealing was going on without the knowledge of his British colleagues. But the head of British Intelligence had been informed of Helliwell's activities.

The Intelligence chief decided not to tell Helliwell what he knew, but instead, sent him on a special mission to a remote city far from his usual route. Helliwell was given a special written introduction to the British spy network in that country. He was delighted at this, for he was sure that now, he was not only trusted, but was also in possession of a lot of new facts to sell to the enemy. Helliwell's introduction read:

> THOMAS HELLIWELL IS SPECIAL MAN AND NEEDS IMMEDIATE SECRET ASSIGNMENT STOP PLACE YOURSELF DIRECTLY ON NEW ORDERS TAKING TACTICAL ROLE UNDER SPECIAL TERMS STOP HELLIWELL'S ORDERS OVER-RIDE THOSE HANDED IN MOSCOW

Not long after Helliwell had arrived in the distant capital, he disappeared, and was never seen or heard of again. Had Thomas Helliwell read his cable-message rather more thoroughly, he might not have been so anxious to go to his new assignment! The British agent simply read the initial letters of each word, and so got an entirely different idea about Helliwell!

Of course, the grille method could have been used, but this would have meant the British agent abroad would have needed another grille just like the original.

Grilles for Transposition Ciphers

There is another type of grille used for sending a transposition cipher, but which allows the sender to jumble up the letters in a particular way simply by writing through the holes in the grille. Grilles like these are made by cutting holes in a piece of cardboard, but the positions of the holes have to be worked out carefully beforehand. A typical grille is shown on the right.

It works by the sender writing the beginning of his message through

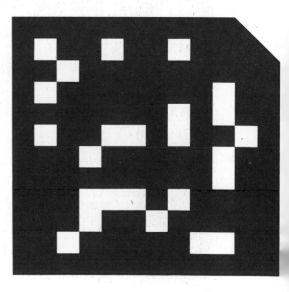

Dear John,

My new sales manager said he wanted to ask you to call on us as soon as you can. However, in the circumstances, it does not seem feasible at present. Henry will come at once if you want complete details of the new plant which we are getting for the factory.

Some more information came regarding the electrical installation, but we do not expect the job to be completed until August, when the new shipping company sends us the specification.

For the time being, we shall rely on the people now operating from our overseas company. There seems to be little time left to investigate reports from all our plants in central Australia but it does appear that nickel-bearing ore is in overseas more to the north.

Forgive a handwritten letter. I am without a typist at present!

Arthur Burrows.

the holes; the grille is then turned on its side, and the message is continued in the new blank spaces. The grille is turned once more, with further letters being written into the new blanks, and finally it is turned a fourth time, and the last of the letters are filled in.

The corner of the grille above has been cut off to help check the correct corner to begin the following quotation from Shakespeare:

> *All the world's a stage,*
> *And all the men and women merely players;*
> *They have their exits and their entrances;*
> *And one man in his time plays many parts.*

The grille is placed at the top left-hand corner of a piece of paper, the cut-off corner positioned at the left. The message is now written in the squares of the grille as below left:

When the grille is removed, the cipher looks like this:

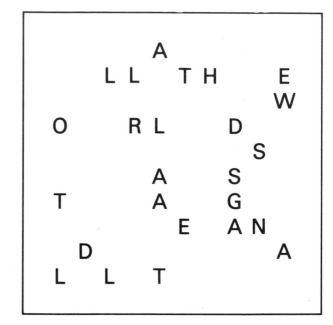

The grille is then rotated, or moved to the second position so that the cut-off corner is now at the right-hand top corner. Continuing with the message, letters are written into the squares as below left:

When the grille is removed, the cipher looks as below:

Once again the grille is rotated, or moved to the right, so that the cut-off corner is now at the bottom right-hand side. Further letters of the message are written, filling up the exposed squares, until it looks as below:

When the grille again is removed, the cipher appears as below:

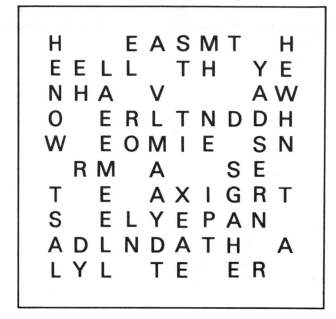

Finally, the grille is rotated so that the cut-off corner is at the bottom left-hand side, and more squares are filled with the message as the picture below left:

When the grille is finally removed, the square looks like that below:

The message, in fact, has not been completed, since the quotation, so far as the cipher is concerned, ends at the word 'his'. To have continued the message would have simply meant beginning a new cipher square.

Another type of grille which can be used for enciphering is called

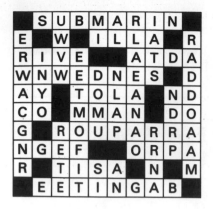

the 'Crossword' cipher. This requires a square, ruled up with black and white smaller squares, so that it looks very much like a blank crossword puzzle. To send the message: SUBMARINE WILL ARRIVE AT DAWN WEDNESDAY TO LAND COMMANDO GROUP ARRANGE FOR PARTISAN MEETING, on the left is a 'crossword' square.

Words of the message have been lettered into the squares, reading across, with any spaces between the words being ignored. The words are then taken from the square, but read downwards, rather than across: ERWACGNR SINYOGE UWVWRETE BEETMOFIT MIDOMUSI ALNLAPAN RLAEANAOG IATSRRNA NDNDRPB RADDOAAM. The cipher message can now only be read by someone who has an identically ruled 'crossword' square. As the message did not quite fill up the squares of the grille, the two 'nulls', A and B, have been added at the end.

All these ciphers have actually been used by spies, by military leaders, and simply by people who wanted to keep their messages secret. Law-breakers, for instance, are among those who are often very anxious to keep secrets. There was a famous case of a bank robber in France, who was caught only six days after the robbery had been committed, yet the police found no trace of the money.

The head of the French Secret Service suspected that the robber, who was known only by the alias 'Pastoure', had hidden the money but had written down somewhere details of its hiding place in cipher, so he sent for a famous cipher expert named André Langie.

It seemed that Pastoure had insisted on making his will soon after being captured. The will appeared quite ordinary for the most part, but the last page was covered with all sorts of figures, which puzzled the head of the Secret Service. Pastoure had assured him that the figures were only his 'working-out' of the private money he had in his own bank. This was possible, for there were all sorts of addition and subtraction sums, multiplication and division, but the Secret Service man suspected that it was some sort of cipher.

Langie examined the will, and decided it was worth a detailed study. He worked at the figures for some time, until at last he found the answer. It *was* a cipher, but the deciphered message was even more mysterious and read,

"*Calvisius, Opus Chronologicum. Bibliothèque Municipale*".

The *Bibliothèque Municipale* is the name of a Paris library, and Langie guessed that the first part of the message referred to the name of a book. He therefore went to the library, and asked for the book by the author Calvisius. The librarian handed him the volume, which was a very large, leather-bound book. Langie expected to find some passages in the book marked in code or cipher; instead he found nothing. Eventually he examined the back inside cover, and noticed that the top corner was creased, and seemed somewhat lumpy. Langie sponged off the creased paper, revealing a carefully made hole, inside which was hidden a small metal key. On the key was the name and number of a safe-deposit, which, when opened later, contained 1,300,000 francs, the proceeds of the robbery committed by Pastoure earlier.

Pastoure's cipher was a substitution cipher, one of the oldest kinds to be used, and which remains the most commonly employed of all ciphers.

Far right: Pastoure

Substitution Ciphers

A *substitution* cipher, instead of simply jumbling up the letters of the original message, replaces or *substitutes* the letters of the message with other letters, figures or symbols. A simple example of this is when the letters of the alphabet are replaced by numbers: A = 1, B = 2, C = 3, D = 4, and so forth. Using this cipher, the message: MEET ME AT THE OLD RUINED TOWER would look like:

13 5 5 20　13 5　1 20　20 8 5　15 12 4　18 21 9 14 5 4
20 15 23 5 18

Obviously this is far too simple for use in any cipher intended to be secret, as it would not take long to discover the key. The cipher can be made much more complicated, or difficult to decipher by altering the figures; for instance, A could equal 15; B = 3; C = 24; D = 18. However, in order to remember which figure equals which letter, a piece of paper would have to be carried showing how the cipher worked. This could mean that the piece of paper could be lost, or it could fall into the wrong hands.

A system which needs no written notes is far better. Julius Caesar used such a cipher but substituted other letters for the ones in the message. He worked by substituting each letter for the one which stood four places further along in the alphabet, so that A = D, B = E, C = F, and so on, still a very simple cipher. Far better to use a keyword, in which every letter is different. Using the word DELIGHT as the keyword, the word is written down with each letter over the top of the first seven letters of the alphabet:

D E L I G H T
A B C D E F G H I J K L M N O P Q R S T U V W X Y Z

The remaining letters of the alphabet, after taking out D, E, L, I, G, H, T, should then be written in order over the top of the full alphabet:

D E L I G H T A B C F J K M N O P Q R S U V W X Y Z
A B C D E F G H I J K L M N O P Q R S T U V W X Y Z

The last six letters of the alphabet remain unchanged when enciphered, which is of little consequence as these six letters are not frequently used. MEET ME AT THE OLD RUINED TOWER in this cipher would appear as:

K G G S　K G　D S　S A G　N J I　Q U B M G I　S N W G Q

Ciphers of this type are usually called 'Julius Caesar' ciphers.

Of course, the letters of the message need not be represented by other letters. Figures, or any kind of symbol can be used instead. The Morse Code, in fact, is a kind of substitution cipher, in which the letters are replaced by various combinations of dots and dashes.

On the left is a set of symbols based on a cipher popularly believed to have been invented by King Solomon.

In the Middle Ages, alchemists and others made up a cipher in which the letters of the alphabet were replaced by signs of the Zodiac and other symbols which looked equally mysterious. However, they are

Solomon's cipher

almost as impractical as King Solomon's cipher, the symbols being difficult to write. This is another cipher based on Chinese numbers. A message in the cipher is written down this page, in Chinese style:

A	= ⊙	= Sun	N	= ♌	= Lion
B	= ♃	= Jupiter	O	= ♍	= Virgo
C	= ♄	= Saturn	P	= ♎	= Balance (Libra)
D	= ♆	= Neptune	Q	= ♏	= Scorpion
E	= ♅	= Uranus	R	= ♐	= Sagittarius
F	= ♁	= Earth	S	= ♑	= Capricorn
G	= ♀	= Venus	T	= ♓	= Fishes
H	= ♂	= Mars	U	= ♈	= Ram
I	= ☿	= Mercury	V	= ♒	= Aquarius
J	= ☽	= Moon	W	= >	
K	= ♉	= Taurus	X	= ≫	
L	= ♊	= Twins	Y	= ⌶	
M	= ♋	= Cancer	Z	= <	

'Chinese' cipher

A B C D E F G H I J K L M N O P

Q R S T U V W X Y Z

During the 16th century, a Neapolitan named Giovanni Porta thought of an ingenious idea for a cipher system, which worked on the basis of the block of letters shown on the right.

In Porta's cipher, the various letters are replaced by a symbol according to the position occupied by that letter. This means that A = ⌐ B = ˙⌐ C = .⌐ D = ⌐ and so on. MY BROTHER JONATHAN in this cipher would look like this:

A	D	G
B•	•E	•H
C•	•F	•I
J	M	P
K•	•N	•Q
L•	•O	•R
S	V	Y
T•	•W	
U•	•X	•Z

The cipher is often called the Freemason's or Rosicrucian cipher, and a rather more popular variation of it looks like this:

Above: Porta's cipher and *below*: Freemason's or Rosicrucian cipher

A	B	C			N•	O•	P•		
D	E	F			Q•	R•	•S		
G	H	I			T•	U•	V		

J K L M

W X Y Z

Here is a message written in the more popular version:

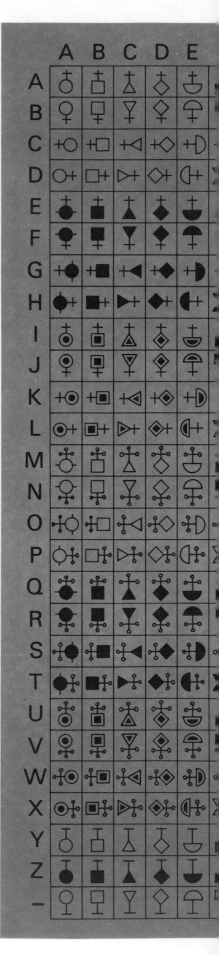

Giovanni Porta, developed other more complicated ciphers than this and the best of them was based on a table like the one shown below:

AB	a	b	c	d	e	f	g	h	i	j	k	l	m
	n	o	p	q	r	s	t	u	v	w	x	y	z

CD	a	b	c	d	e	f	g	h	i	j	k	l	m
	z	n	o	p	q	r	s	t	u	v	w	x	y

EF	a	b	c	d	e	f	g	h	i	j	k	l	m
	y	z	n	o	p	q	r	s	t	u	v	w	x

GH	a	b	c	d	e	f	g	h	i	j	k	l	m
	x	y	z	n	o	p	q	r	s	t	u	v	w

IJ	a	b	c	d	e	f	g	h	i	j	k	l	m
	w	x	y	z	n	o	p	q	r	s	t	u	v

KL	a	b	c	d	e	f	g	h	i	j	k	l	m
	v	w	x	y	z	n	o	p	q	r	s	t	u

MN	a	b	c	d	e	f	g	h	i	j	k	l	m
	u	v	w	x	y	z	n	o	p	q	r	s	t

OP	a	b	c	d	e	f	g	h	i	j	k	l	m
	t	u	v	w	x	y	z	n	o	p	q	r	s

QR	a	b	c	d	e	f	g	h	i	j	k	l	m
	s	t	u	v	w	x	y	z	n	o	p	q	r

ST	a	b	c	d	e	f	g	h	i	j	k	l	m
	r	s	t	u	v	w	x	y	z	n	o	p	q

UV	a	b	c	d	e	f	g	h	i	j	k	l	m
	q	r	s	t	u	v	w	x	y	z	n	o	p

WX	a	b	c	d	e	f	g	h	i	j	k	l	m
	p	q	r	s	t	u	v	w	x	y	z	n	o

YZ	a	b	c	d	e	f	g	h	i	j	k	l	m
	o	p	q	r	s	t	u	v	w	x	y	z	n

The Porta table was thought by many, including the great Napoleon Buonaparte, to be very secret. Buonaparte used it for his private correspondence. It is very well known now, of course, but still very baffling to someone not in the secret. To work the cipher a key-

46

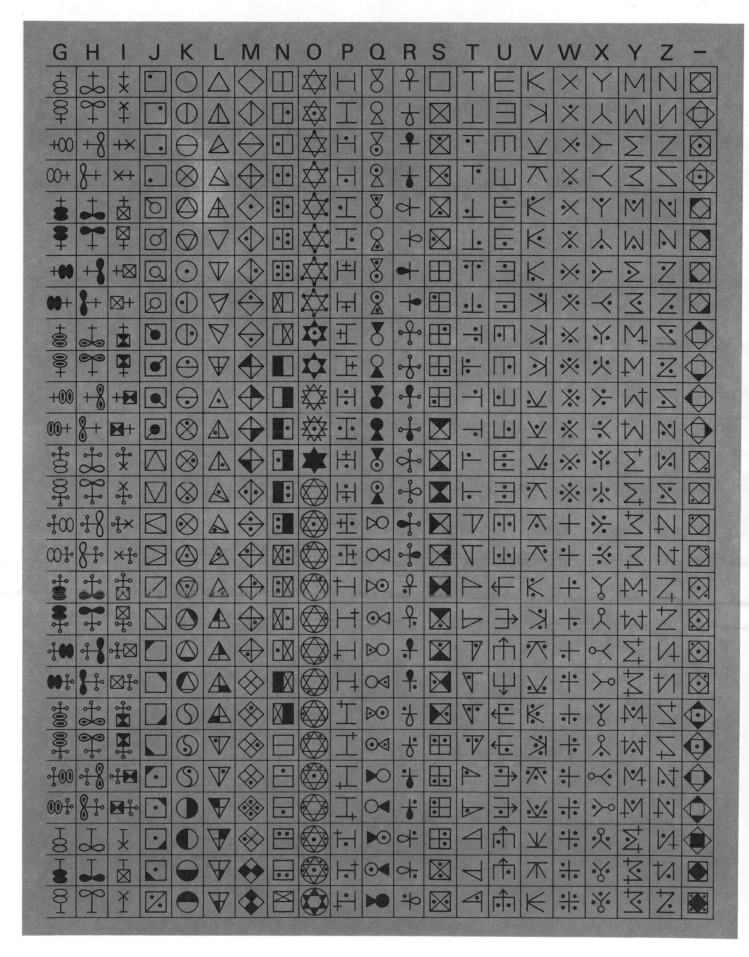

word or phrase is first chosen, i.e. RULE BRITANNIA. To encipher the following message: THE ENGLISH CHANNEL IS TO BE CROSSED BY A FLEET OF TWENTY-FOUR WARSHIPS the message is written out, with the key-phrase repeated over and over at the top of the letters, omitting spaces and punctuation.

R U L E B R I T A N N I A R U L E B R I T A N N I A R U L E
T H E E N G L I S H C H A N N E L I S T O B E C R O S S E D

B R I T A N N I A R U L E B R I T A N N I A R U L E B R
B Y A F L E E T O F T W E N T Y F O U R W A R S H I P S

The first letter of the key-phrase is R, which is found in the first upright column of the Porta table on page 46. The first letter of the *message* is T. R shares a row with Q (QR). Looking along this row for T, it is found standing below the letter b and b now becomes the first letter of the cipher message. The next letter of the key-phrase is U, which shares a row with V (UV) in the first upright column of the table. Along this row, is the next message-letter, H. The H stands above x, which becomes the next letter of the cipher. The message should be continued, until the cipher, when completed, looks like this: BXZPA YUZFO WQNIK ZWVAK KOYWI BACZO OGWWY YYKBX DBPAB CWBAK ANMCP TCA.

As is usual, the final cipher has been split into five-letter groups. The last group of letters in the message is three, and two nulls must be added and enciphered bringing the group up to five letters again.

To decipher the message the whole procedure is reversed. Using the same cipher, but with the keyword MANCHESTER, the cipher message is VRIFO ERAPV. The keyword is first written down, and beneath it, each letter of the cipher message:

M A N C H E S T E R
V R I F O E R A P V

The first keyword letter is M, which appears in the first upright column marked MN row. Along this row is the first letter of the cipher, which is V. V stands below B, which is the first letter of the deciphered, or 'clear' message. Next is keyletter A, also in the first column, sharing a place with B; in other words, the AB row. In this row, is the cipher letter R, which stands below E, the second letter of the clear message. Continuing in this way, the complete phrase is BE PREPARED.

Giovanni Porta invented a number of ciphers, and one which looked very strange indeed was similar to the table on page 46, but with symbols instead of letters. On page 47 is a modern version of Porta's symbol table, or chart.

To send a message in Porta's symbol cipher, one must first write down the whole message, but split it up into pairs: ME ET ME AT TH ER UI NE DT OW ER (Meet me at the ruined tower). The first two letters, being ME, are found down the left-hand side of the chart for M, and along the top of the chart for the letter E. The lines are then traced across and down until they meet. The symbol in this square is . The next pair of letters is ET. E and T cross at the square bearing the symbol ⊥, which is followed by the pair ME again. The same method is followed throughout, until the complete message is enciphered. It will then look like this:

One of the very earliest forms of cipher was invented in 1518 by a Benedictine monk called Trithemius, or Tritheim. His system was to replace each *letter* of a message by a special code word, so that when the message was written out, it read quite differently, if somewhat strangely. Trithemius worked with fourteen different alphabets, so that each letter of the message had to be enciphered from a different alphabet.

Despite its complicated appearance, the alphabetic cipher of Trithemius was a substitution one, but one letter could be replaced by as many as 14 variations. Not only was the cipher difficult to use, but a cumbersome alphabetic table had also to be carried.

One man who worked out a simple way of varying the letters which were substituted for the original message was a Frenchman named Blaise de Vigenère, who published a large book detailing his ideas. His system, which was really an improvement upon Porta's table, is based on what is now known as the Vigenère table.

Vigenère table

	A	B	C	D	E	F	G	H	I	J	K	L	M	N	O	P	Q	R	S	T	U	V	W	X	Y	Z
A	a	b	c	d	e	f	g	h	i	j	k	l	m	n	o	p	q	r	s	t	u	v	w	x	y	z
B	b	c	d	e	f	g	h	i	j	k	l	m	n	o	p	q	r	s	t	u	v	w	x	y	z	a
C	c	d	e	f	g	h	i	j	k	l	m	n	o	p	q	r	s	t	u	v	w	x	y	z	a	b
D	d	e	f	g	h	i	j	k	l	m	n	o	p	q	r	s	t	u	v	w	x	y	z	a	b	c
E	e	f	g	h	i	j	k	l	m	n	o	p	q	r	s	t	u	v	w	x	y	z	a	b	c	d
F	f	g	h	i	j	k	l	m	n	o	p	q	r	s	t	u	v	w	x	y	z	a	b	c	d	e
G	g	h	i	j	k	l	m	n	o	p	q	r	s	t	u	v	w	x	y	z	a	b	c	d	e	f
H	h	i	j	k	l	m	n	o	p	q	r	s	t	u	v	w	x	y	z	a	b	c	d	e	f	g
I	i	j	k	l	m	n	o	p	q	r	s	t	u	v	w	x	y	z	a	b	c	d	e	f	g	h
J	j	k	l	m	n	o	p	q	r	s	t	u	v	w	x	y	z	a	b	c	d	e	f	g	h	i
K	k	l	m	n	o	p	q	r	s	t	u	v	w	x	y	z	a	b	c	d	e	f	g	h	i	j
L	l	m	n	o	p	q	r	s	t	u	v	w	x	y	z	a	b	c	d	e	f	g	h	i	j	k
M	m	n	o	p	q	r	s	t	u	v	w	x	y	z	a	b	c	d	e	f	g	h	i	j	k	l
N	n	o	p	q	r	s	t	u	v	w	x	y	z	a	b	c	d	e	f	g	h	i	j	k	l	m
O	o	p	q	r	s	t	u	v	w	x	y	z	a	b	c	d	e	f	g	h	i	j	k	l	m	n
P	p	q	r	s	t	u	v	w	x	y	z	a	b	c	d	e	f	g	h	i	j	k	l	m	n	o
Q	q	r	s	t	u	v	w	x	y	z	a	b	c	d	e	f	g	h	i	j	k	l	m	n	o	p
R	r	s	t	u	v	w	x	y	z	a	b	c	d	e	f	g	h	i	j	k	l	m	n	o	p	q
S	s	t	u	v	w	x	y	z	a	b	c	d	e	f	g	h	i	j	k	l	m	n	o	p	q	r
T	t	u	v	w	x	y	z	a	b	c	d	e	f	g	h	i	j	k	l	m	n	o	p	q	r	s
U	u	v	w	x	y	z	a	b	c	d	e	f	g	h	i	j	k	l	m	n	o	p	q	r	s	t
V	v	w	x	y	z	a	b	c	d	e	f	g	h	i	j	k	l	m	n	o	p	q	r	s	t	u
W	w	x	y	z	a	b	c	d	e	f	g	h	i	j	k	l	m	n	o	p	q	r	s	t	u	v
X	x	y	z	a	b	c	d	e	f	g	h	i	j	k	l	m	n	o	p	q	r	s	t	u	v	w
Y	y	z	a	b	c	d	e	f	g	h	i	j	k	l	m	n	o	p	q	r	s	t	u	v	w	x
Z	z	a	b	c	d	e	f	g	h	i	j	k	l	m	n	o	p	q	r	s	t	u	v	w	x	y

To encipher the following message: ENEMY ADVANCING ON BOTH FLANKS SEND HELP AT ONCE

A keyword must first be chosen. This can be any word as long as the letters are all different. Using the keyword SIMPLE this is written over and over again along the top of the message:

S I M P L E S I M P L E S I M P L E S I M P L E S I M P L E S I M P L E S I M P
E N E M Y A D V A N C I N G O N B O T H F L A N K S S E N D H E L P A T O N C E

To encipher, find in the top row of the Vigenère table the first letter of the message, which is E. The letter of the keyword is S, which can be found in the *vertical* column. Next, one line should be traced along the vertical line from E in the top row and one along the horizontal line from S, until the two rows meet. The meeting point is at the letter W in the table.

This is the first letter of the enciphered message. The next letter of the original is N, of which the key-letter is I. Again in the top horizontal row is N, and in the vertical alphabet is I, the two rows meeting at the letter V – the second letter of the cipher. Continuing in this manner right through the message, the final cipher looks like this:

Keyword repeated S I M P L E S I M P L E S I M P L E S I M P L E S I M P L E S I M P L E S I M P
'Clear' message   E N E M Y A D V A N C I N G O N B O T H F L A N K S S E N D H E L P A T O N C E
Cipher   W V Q B J E V I M C N M F O A C M S L P R A L R C A E T Y H Z M X E L X G V O T

The cipher is very unwieldy as it stands, so for convenience, it is split into five-letter groups:

WVQBJ EVIMC NMFOA CMSLP RALRC AETYH ZMXEL XGVOT

Vigenère's cipher is called 'polyalphabetic', because it uses many alphabets to represent the original message. Comparing the cipher message with the original, it can be seen that, for instance, E is represented sometimes by W, sometimes by Q, or sometimes by T or M. The same applies to the other letters, each of which appears in the cipher message represented by several other letters.

To decipher, the person receiving the message writes the keyword SIMPLE over the cipher, repeating it as many times as necessary. Then he looks for the letter of the keyword at the top of the table. In this case it is S. He runs down that column until he finds the first letter of the cipher, which is W. To the left of the line in the first column is the letter E (shown in capital letters), the first letter of the deciphered message. The decipherment then continues in this way.

This system can also be worked out by using a slide composed of two alphabets like the one shown in the picture:

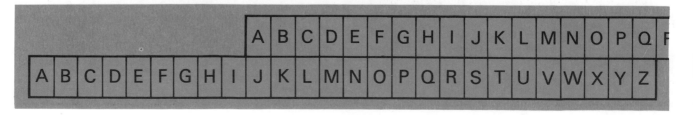

Bacon's Cipher

Francis Bacon, who lived nearly four hundred years ago, was very interested in codes and ciphers, and invented a number of ingenious ones, which baffled most people at the time. Because of this interest of Bacon's, some people have claimed to have seen secret ciphers in the early editions of Shakespeare's plays, and the messages, when deciphered, proved to them to have been written by Francis Bacon himself. It is not a very convincing theory, but it does involve an interesting cipher used by Francis Bacon.

He had noticed that many printed books in those days had wrongly positioned, or badly printed letters, or used letters taken from a different fount of type. Printers in those days were very careless, and Bacon decided to base a cipher on this fact. First, he wrote out a table like this:

A	B	C	D	E	F	G	H	I&J
aaaaa	aaaab	aaaba	aaabb	aabaa	aabab	aabba	aabbb	abaaa
K	L	M	N	O	P	Q	R	S
abaab	ababa	ababb	abbaa	abbab	abbba	abbbb	baaaa	baaab
T	U&V	W	X	Y	Z			
baaba	baabb	babaa	babab	babba	babbb			

In the days of Francis Bacon, people used U and V, and I and J interchangeably, so Bacon did not use separate symbols for them. Bacon's

Francis Bacon

idea was to use this system to hide a message in a page of printed type, or even in something written by hand.

The message could be hidden in various ways: by deliberately setting the type in a special way; by marking certain letters with a pen, or even by pricking holes in those letters. There is something 'odd' about the following passage. Certain letters have been set in heavier type than the ordinary roman characters:

The **qu**ality of **m**er**cy is not s**train'**d**;
It droppet**h as the** gentle **rain** from heaven
Upo**n** th**e** place beneath: **it** is **twice** bless'd;
It blesseth **h**im that **gives** and him that **takes**:
'Tis **mightiest in the mig**htiest; **it** becomes
The throned monarch better than **his crown**.

In fact, the passage – which is Portia's speech from Shakespeare's *The Merchant of Venice* – hides a message in Baconian cipher. It is easier to decipher the passage by first writing out the passage in capital letters, in five-letter groups, ignoring all punctuation and similar marks, underlining all the letters which appear in the heavier type:

THEQU ALITY OFMER CYISN OTSTR AINDI
TDROP PETHA STHEG ENTLE RAINF ROMHE
AVENU PONTH EPLAC EBENE ATHIT ISTWI
CEBLE SSDIT BLESS ETHHI MTHAT GIVES
ANDHI MTHAT TAKES TISMI GHTIE STINT
HEMIG HTIES TITBE COMES THETH RONED
MONAR CHBET TERTH ANHIS CROWN

The first group of five letters is THEQU. Ignoring the actual letters used, and writing a small 'a' for each letter not underlined and a small 'b' for each underlined letter gives us 'aaaab'.

Checking the table above, 'aaab' is the equivalent of the letter B. The next group, ALITY, has no underlined letter in it, so it represents 'aaaaa'. The table above shows that this is equivalent to the letter A. The first two letters of the message are, therefore, BA.

The next group is OFMER, which, written out in small 'a's and 'b's, is 'aaaba', and according to the table, is equivalent to C. Following this system throughout the passage, it is simple to decipher the message, but the answer appears on page 72.

The Voynich Manuscript

By a strange coincidence, another man named Bacon – Roger Bacon, scientist and philosopher – was also interested in codes and ciphers, as was discovered during the early part of this century.

In 1912, an American dealer in books and manuscripts, Doctor Wilfrid Voynich, bought a box filled with old manuscripts and documents while in Italy and which he hoped to sell in the United States. One manuscript was rather odd looking, and Voynich, despite his experience, was quite unable to read it. It seemed to be in no known language, but Voynich was able to discover that the manuscript was the work of Roger Bacon, who lived from 1214 until 1292 A.D.

Voynich took copies of his manuscript, and showed them to various experts on old documents, as well as to scholars experienced in deciphering ancient inscriptions. To his astonishment, not a single person was able to make anything of the manuscript, which, at first glance, looked as if it had been written in a mediaeval version of Latin or Greek.

Yet the characters were not from either of those alphabets. The whole work was in *cipher*, cleverly written in the hand of Roger Bacon over seven hundred years before. Since that time, numerous cryptographers have tried their hand at deciphering the Voynich manuscript, but without success. Bacon's cipher was unbreakable, and so it has proved until this day.

Cipher-wheels and Slides

These are called St Cyr slides, and the order of the letters shown can be varied. Another way of getting a similar result is by the use of a cipher wheel. You can make one yourself, and instructions for doing this are given at the end of this book.

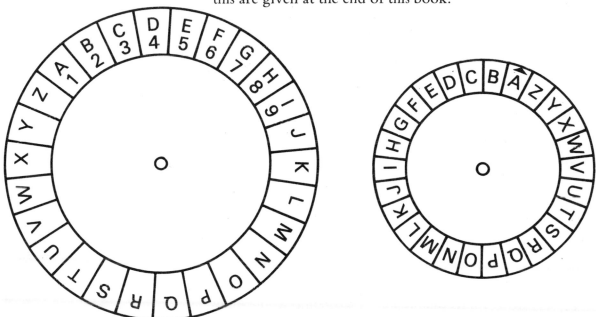

To use the cipher-wheel, and to encipher a message, a key-number must first be chosen. Using 1973 as an example the message to encipher can be the same as before: ENEMY ADVANCING ON BOTH FLANKS SEND HELP AT ONCE and should be written down with the key-number over the top:

1 9 7 3 1 9 7 3 1 9 7 3 1 9 7 3 1 9 7 3 1 9 7 3 1 9 7 3 1 9 7 3 1 9 7 3 1 9 7 3
E N E M Y A D V A N C I N G O N B O T H F L A N K S S E N D H E L P A T O N C E

Taking the cipher-wheel, the inner disc should be turned until the small arrow is opposite the first figure of the key-number, which is 1. Look for the first letter of our message on the inner disc: the letter is E, and opposite, on the largest disc is the letter W, which is the first letter of the enciphered message.

The disc should then be turned so that the arrow is opposite the next figure of the key-number (9). The next letter of the message is N, and opposite is V, the second letter of the cipher. Turning the disc to bring the arrow opposite 7, look for the next letter, which is E again, and opposite C. The arrow is then turned to 3, and opposite M is Q.

Continue in this way until the cipher is completed. The cipher will look like this:

Key-number	1 9 7 3	1 9 7 3	1 9 7 3	1 9 7 3	1 9 7 3	1 9 7 3	1 9 7 3	1 9 7 3	1 9 7 3	1 9 7 3
Message	E N E M	Y A D V	A N C I	N G O N	B O T H	F L A N K	S S E N	D H E L	P A T O	N C E
Cipher	W V C Q	C I D H	A V E U	N C S P	Z U N V	V X G P	Q Q O Y	N F Z Y	P T G J	M V E Y

Finally, the message is once again split into five-letter groups: WVCQC IDHAV EUNCS PZUNV VXGPQ QOYNF ZYPTG JMVEY. To send messages the recipient must of course have a cipher-wheel just like the sender's. To decipher the message, the whole procedure is reversed, but whoever does this must know the key-number.

Books Written in Cipher

Many famous people have tried to keep their work secret by means of ciphers. One of these was Leonardo da Vinci, whose notebooks contained minute details of many novel ideas. Together with drawings, the notebooks explained Leonardo's ideas for such advanced things as flying machines and armoured fighting vehicles. The reason for his secrecy was that in those days, anyone putting forward such outlandish notions was highly suspect, and Leonardo had no wish to be accused of witchcraft, or having dealings with the devil.

Leonardo da Vinci

Not only did Leonardo take the precaution of writing his notes in a form of Greek, but he also wrote them in 'mirror' writing, which required the whole work to be held in front of a looking glass before it could be read.

General Henri-Gatien Bertrand, Napoleon's friend, who spent years of imprisonment with Napoleon on the island of St. Helena, kept a secret diary of the French emperor's life there. Bertrand wrote in such an abbreviated type of French that it amounted to a cipher, and it took a special interpreter to transcribe the diary into ordinary French.

Samuel Pepys, the famous and well published English diarist, had no intention of publishing his work. It was intended to be secret, and in order to prevent anyone from reading it, Pepys wrote the whole diary in a form of shorthand, long since forgotten. The diary was written during the years 1660–1669, and covered over three thousand detailed pages. For over 150 years, Pepys's diary held its secret, and then, in the early years of the 19th century, Thomas Grenville, a book collector, began an attempt at deciphering it.

Samuel Pepys

Grenville's work was continued by a Cambridge scholar, the Reverend John Smith, who had realised that Pepys had used a system of shorthand invented by Thomas Shelton in the 17th century. In fact, Shelton had invented two systems, one in 1641 and one in 1650. Both were forms of cipher, in which the letters were simplified outlines, substituted for the ordinary ones. Thomas Shelton's systems of shorthand were based on the following letters:

A	B	C	D	E	F	G	H	I	J	K	L	M	N	O	P	Q	R	S	T	U	V	W	X	Y	Z	
∧	I	Γ	⌐	♂	⊐	ᒣ	Ч	<	L	L	∩	∪	—	(	σ	٩	ρ	/	∨	∨	∨	X	Y	Z	(1st)
<	∧	⌐	\	e	L	∧	O	Γ	∧	(	—	)	/	∪	ρ	٩	r	σ	I	∨	∨	(	⋎	⋎	Z	(2nd)

54

John Smith completed his work of decipherment in 1825, revealing many startling details of life in the late 17th century. Pepys probably felt he needed to keep his diary private during his lifetime. No doubt he remembered that when he was a young man, there were many who used ciphers in matters of life and death. Those were during the days Cromwell ruled England, when opponents to the government were arrested and thrown in prison.

One such man was Sir John Trevanion, a cavalier, who was caught and thrown into a dungeon in Colchester Castle. Already, a number of Sir John's friends had been tried and sentenced to death, and he had no doubt that he, too, would shortly follow them to a similar fate.

However, Sir John was able to receive letters from friends, and one day, his gaoler handed him a letter, which reads as follows:

Oliver Cromwell

Worthie Sir John: Hope, that is the beste comfort of the afflicted, cannot much, I fear me, help you now. That I would saye to you, is this only: if ever I may be able to requite that I do owe you, stand not upon asking me. 'Tis not much I can do: but what I can do, bee you verie sure I wille. I knowe that, if dethe comes, if ordinary men fear it, it frights not you, accounting it for a high honour, to have such a rewarde of your loyalty. Pray yet that you may be spared this soe bitter, cup. I fear not that you will grudge any sufferings; onlie if bie submission you can turn them away, 'tis the part of a wise man. Tell me, as if you can, to do for you any thinge that you wolde have done. The general goes back on Wednesday. Restinge your servant to command.

R.T.

Sir John Trevanion seemed more than usually interested in this letter, and later in the day asked if he might be taken to the prison chapel to pray and meditate. Naturally, such a request could hardly be refused. In any case, the chapel was quite secure, having only one door, while the windows were small, narrow and set very high in the walls. Since Sir John wished to pray, the guard, believing the chapel to be secure, left him alone for a while.

Sir John seemed to be spending some time in his prayers, and at last, the gaolers grew suspicious. They went back into the chapel, only to find the place empty, without a sign of their prisoner. Sir John Trevanion had escaped as a result of a secret message concealed in the words of the letter. Obviously, the cipher had been arranged previously with a friend.

Had the guards been more clever, they, too, could have discovered the secret of the letter. All they had to do was to read the third letter after each mark of punctuation. The 'clear' message would then have been:

PANEL AT EAST END OF CHAPEL SLIDES.

Napoleon Buonaparte

The Zig-Zag Cipher
During the First World War, spies were numerous in all the Allied countries, but the problem was, as always, to discover their identity. In those days, radio had not been developed but spies still had to get their information out of the country, and this was often their undoing. All sorts of clever tricks were used, and the spy-catchers were on the

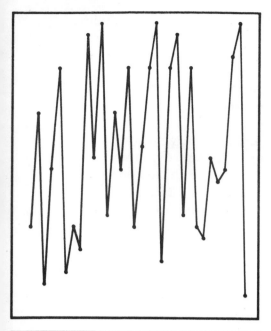

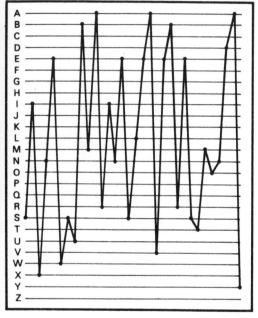

watch for them. One woman in France, an expert needlewoman, had for years sold her work to a firm in Switzerland, which was a neutral country. During the war, she continued to send her samples to the Swiss town.

It was a matter of routine for her parcels to be opened and examined by the French authorities, but since they contained only samples of fine embroidery, they were sent on to their destination in Switzerland. Unfortunately, a counter-espionage agent one day had a closer look at the woman's embroidery. She seemed to be particularly fond of a zig-zag pattern, which was often quite haphazard in appearance.

The agent felt there was something unusual about it, and spent some time studying the embroidery, until at last he hit upon the solution. The embroidery itself was sewn in such a way as to make up a cipher message, and when discovered, it was quite simple to read. The woman, of course, was later arrested, and the flow of information ceased. On the left is an example of a message sent by the woman.

The cipher expert traced the pattern carefully on to a piece of paper, and ruled lines across the page like this so it looked like the second sketch on the left.

Then he lettered the alphabet down the horizontal columns as shown. He decided that the points where the lines ended signified the letter shown against that column, and he soon came up with this message:

SIX NEW SUBMARINES LEAVE BREST MONDAY

The same system can be used in various other ways, such as on a fake sales graph. It would look, to the casual eye, like an ordinary sales chart, because the cipher would be hidden in the 'up-and-down' lines.

Shopkeepers, particularly those keeping antique shops, sometimes put mysterious-looking labels on their goods, which otherwise have nothing to show the price. Prospective buyers, seeing a ticket attached to, perhaps, a grandfather clock, might find it marked 'ghij'. There may be even another set of letters. These are the shopkeeper's own private note of the amount he originally paid for the article.

One buyer who was interested in old clocks was also a keen amateur cryptographer, and he chanced upon an English dealer named Blandish who showed his prices in this way. The buyer made several trips to the shop, each time making a note of the prices, and also the code letters shown on the price ticket. At last, he decided he had enough to work on, and made a list of various items:

	Price shown	Code letters
Oil painting	£50.00	br
Table	£25.00	en
Snuff box	£5.50	l.br
Chiming clock	£12.25	n.nr
Paper knife, silver	£2.50	e.rr
Barometer	£4.75	b.rr
Antique tea set	£16.00	h.nr

The buyer guessed that the code letters showed what the dealer had originally paid, and he also guessed that the letters after the full stops showed pence. The number of times that the letter R was repeated suggested that R might equal O, so that N probably equalled 5.

Suddenly, he had an idea. The dealer's name was R. E. Blandish, and this had the right number of letters to equal the figures 1, 2, 3, 4, 5, 6, 7, 8 and 9. So, he wrote them down as shown on the right.

The guess proved correct, and the buyer soon knew how much the dealer had paid for the chiming clock in which he was interested. So, instead of paying what the dealer had asked–£12.25–he paid only £10, after a long haggle. It was, of course, a simple substitution cipher and one that can be easily worked out. See if you can discover how much the dealer paid for the clock. The answer appears on page 72.

```
0 1 2 3 4 5 6 7 8 9
R E B L A N D I S H
```

Ciphers in Stories and Films

Ciphers have been used in a number of books and stories, and one of the best known is that deciphered by Sherlock Holmes in Sir Arthur Conan Doyle's short story, *The Dancing Men,* which appears in the collection called *The Return of Sherlock Holmes.* The cipher took the form of a series of little pin-men figures, each of which represented a letter, and which was successfully deciphered by Holmes.

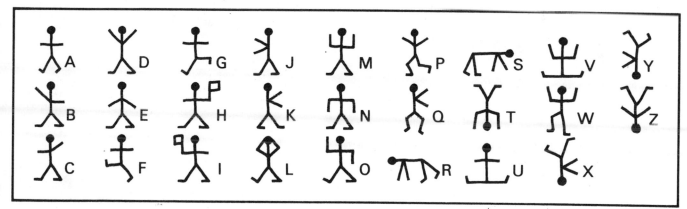

It would be a pity to give the solution to the cipher here lest it should spoil the story, but here is an alphabet of pin-men, made up in a similar way to that found in Conan Doyle's book:

And here is a message, written in the cipher, which, as will be seen quickly, is a simple substitution one.

Other ciphers can be found in several other well-known books. Jules Verne's *The Giant Raft* contains one, and so does his other book, *A Journey to the Centre of the Earth*, in which Professor Lidenbrock discovers the secret tunnel into the earth by solving a cipher in an old document.

Edgar Allan Poe, in his story *The Gold Bug*, uses a cipher in which a successful decipherment leads to the discovery of a fabulous treasure left by Captain Kidd the pirate. Maurice Leblanc, the French writer, and creator of the detective Arsène Lupin, employs a cipher in his novel *The Hollow Needle*, which leads Arsène Lupin on the track of the secret of the Needle itself.

In a film made in 1931 called *Dishonoured*, Marlene Dietrich plays a beautiful spy who sends secret messages simply by playing the piano. The cipher is made up of musical notes, and although such a system is perfectly simple to devise, it is unlikely whether the 'music' would sound very tuneful! However, on the next page is an alphabet which makes use of musical notes.

A Journey to the Centre of the Earth

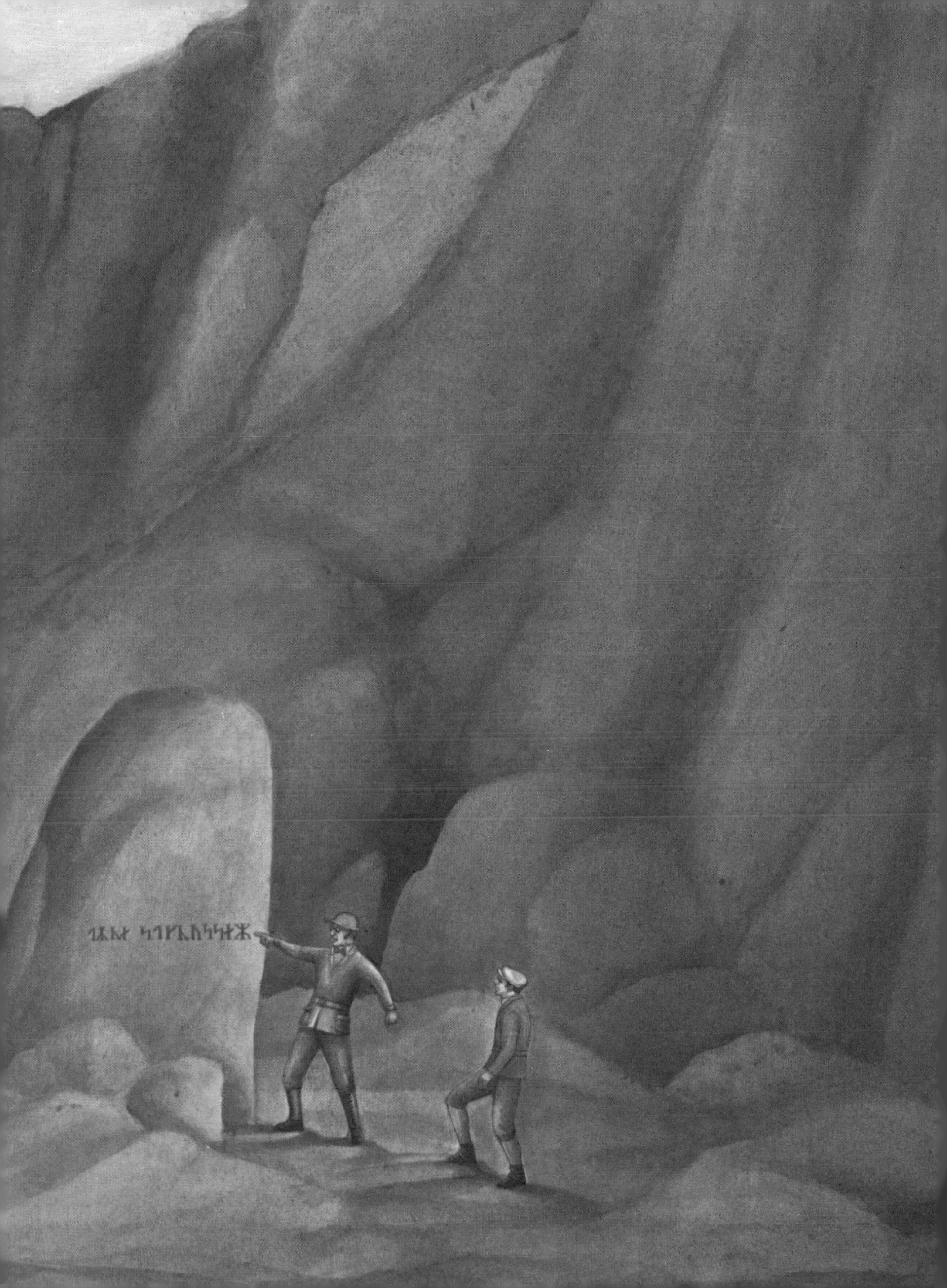

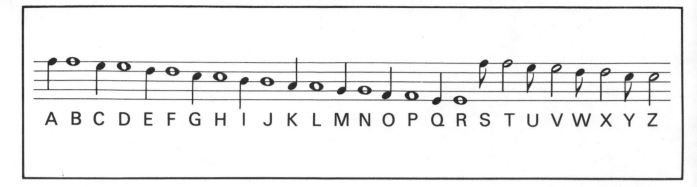

A B C D E F G H I J K L M N O P Q R S T U V W X Y Z

Other books in which ciphers have been used include *Colonel Quaritch, Q.V.,* by Sir Henry Rider Haggard; *The Four Suspects,* by Agatha Christie; *Trent's Last Case,* by E. C. Bentley; *The History of Henry Esmond,* by William Thackeray; *The Tracer of Lost Persons,* by Robert W. Chambers; *Have His Carcase,* by Dorothy L. Sayers; *The Mystery of the Sea,* by Bram Stoker; and *The Hand of Fu Manchu,* by Sax Rohmer. Beatrix Potter, the artist and author of delightful small books for children, herself kept a secret diary in cipher.

The Playfair Cipher

Probably the best of all substitution ciphers is the one called the Playfair cipher, which for some time was on the secret list, since it was used by the British Army, particularly during the Boer War in South Africa. The cipher was worked out as early as 1854 by the famous British inventor, Sir Charles Wheatstone, but it was his friend Lyon Playfair (Lord Playfair), who introduced it to the authorities, and so the cipher was named after him.

It is well worth learning how to work out a Playfair cipher, although it is a little more difficult to grasp than some of the more simple ones. The first thing to do is to choose a keyword, of which the letters must all be different: that is, no letter should be used more than once. Using the keyword CHARLES, the first step is to draw out a square, divided into twenty-five smaller squares as shown on the left.

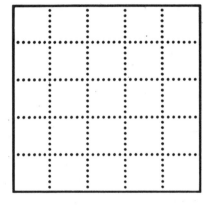

The letters of the keyword should be written into the square like this:

C H A R L
E S . . .
. . . . .
. . . . .
. . . . .

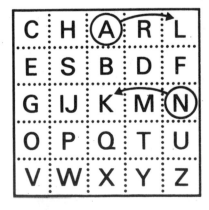

The other squares are now filled up with the remaining letters of the alphabet not contained in the keyword CHARLES:

C H A R L
E S B D F
G I/J K M N
O P Q T U
V W X Y Z

As there are 26 letters in the alphabet, and only 25 squares, one letter is dropped, allowing only one square for I and J. To encipher

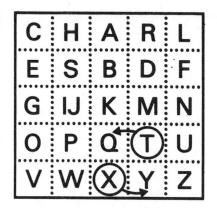

the message, IMPORTANT THAT YOU COME AT ONCE, firstly divide the whole message into two-letter groups. Should a double letter occur in any two-letter group (such as TT where the word 'important' comes before the word 'that'), the letters should be divided by an X. The two-letter grouping should then look like this:

IM PO RT AN TX TH AT YO UC OM EA TO NC EX

A 'null' has been added to the last letter to make up the final pair. It is important to learn the rules, which may appear a little complicated at first:

1. Each pair of letters must be replaced by another pair.
2. When a double letter occurs, such as TT in the message, they must be divided by an X.
3. When the pair of letters from the message appear in the same row of the square, the pair to their *right* becomes the correct cipher letters. For example IM becomes KN, PO becomes QP.
4. When the pair of letters from the message appears in the same column, then the pair *below* are the cipher letters. For example, RT becomes DY.
5. When the letters of the pair are not in the same column, nor in the same row, then the cipher letters are those in the opposite corners of the rectangle containing the message letters. (The letter that comes first in the new pair is the one in the same row as the first letter of the old pair.) For example, AN = LK, TX = QY, and TH = PR.

To encipher the message:
IM PO RT AN TX TH AT YO UC OM EA TO NC EX
KN QP DY LK QY PR RQ VT OL TG BC UP GL BV

This is now written out in five-letter groups:
KNQPD YLKQY PRRQV TOLTG BCUPG LBVXY

Here is another message to encipher, using the same square as before and CHARLES as the keyword: THE CHURCH BELL TOLLS AT NINE.

First step: Message split into two-letter groups:
TH EC HU RC HB EL LT OL LS AT NI NE

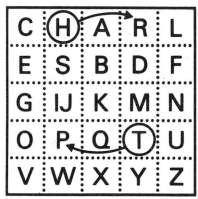

Original message
Cipher letters

Final cipher-message, with two 'nulls' added to complete the last five-letter group.

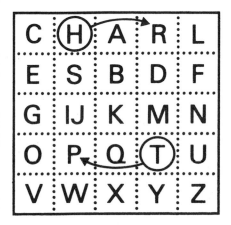

Second step: TH = PR

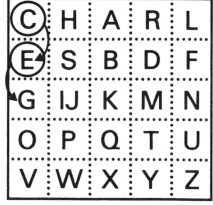

Third step: EC = GE

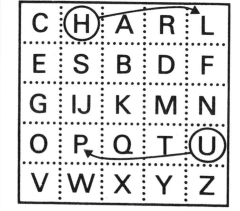

Fourth step: HU = LP

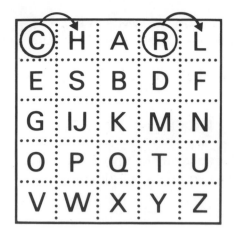

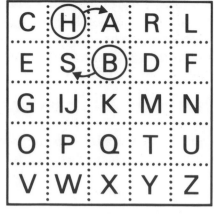

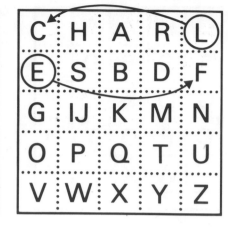

Fifth step: RC = LH

Sixth step: HB = AS

Seventh step: EL = FC

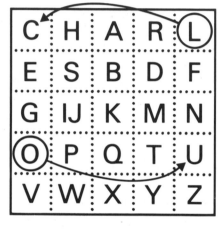

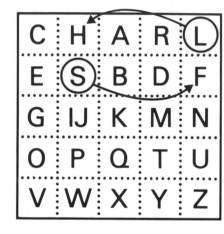

Eighth step: LT = RU

Ninth step: OL = UC

Tenth step: LS = HF

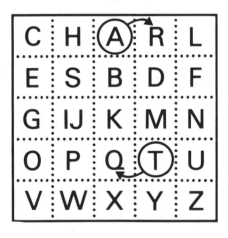

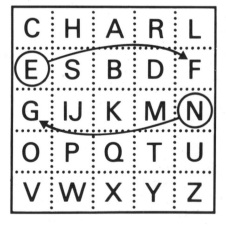

11th step: AT = RQ

12th step: NI = GK

13th step: NE = GF

Now the message looks like this:
TH EC HU RC HB EL LT OL LS AT NI NE

PR GE LP LH AS FC RU UC HF RQ GK GF

This is now written out in five-letter groups:
PRGEL PLHAS   FCRUU CHFRQ GKGFX

Original message in
two-letter groups

Cipher letters

One 'null', X,
added to complete
last group.

62

Invisible Inks

Whether a message is sent in cipher, code or ordinary writing, one of the favourite ways of hiding a message has always been by the use of invisible inks. These are often known as sympathetic inks, because they need some *sympathetic* medium such as a chemical, or simply heat, to make them visible.

The important thing about the use of an invisible ink is that there should be no sign of a message until the paper has been correctly treated to make the writing visible. One of the problems of writing such a secret message is that an ordinary steel nib will show scratch marks, and the writing can often be read by simply holding the paper at a convenient angle to the light, or by brushing fine powder over it.

It is much better for the message to be written with a quill pen. Although quill pens are rarely used nowadays, it is possible to make a quill by using a feather from a large bird such as a goose or a turkey. A sharp knife or pair of scissors should be used to cut the end of the quill to an oblique angle; a short slit should then be made at the point, which should then be trimmed off to form a narrow, but square, end.

A favourite invisible ink, once used by spies the world over, is made with a mixture of cobalt chloride and gum arabic. A solution of this will make an ink which, when first used, will appear pale green in colour. Gradually, the green colour will disappear, and the message will become quite invisible. When heated, however, the message reappears, in a bright blue colour.

A similar ink, but which becomes green on being heated, is made with a mixture of cobalt chloride and nickel chloride in solution. Copper sulphate can also be used, but needs another chemical to 'develop' the message. To make this last-named ink, a teaspoonful of copper sulphate crystals should be added to half a pint of water. It is best, of course, to make rather less than this, reducing the ingredients accordingly. Too much copper sulphate will result in the message being slightly visible when written, since the chemical itself is greenish-blue in colour.

A weak solution of copper sulphate, used as an invisible ink, can also be developed by holding the message over a bottle of ordinary smelling salts. The message can then be caused to disappear again by applying very gentle heat.

When the message is dry, it should be brushed with a solution of ordinary washing soda (sodium carbonate) – about two teaspoonfuls to a half-pint of water. The message will then appear.

Another type of secret ink can be made which is visible when first written, but which gradually fades and finally, after about four days, disappears altogether. To make this ink, a pinch of arrowroot is boiled in a quarter of a pint of water. When the mixture is cold, about a quarter of a teaspoonful of iodine should be added. The ink may vary a little in quality, depending upon the amount of each ingredient used.

Secret messages sent in invisible ink are usually written between the lines of a genuine message or letter, so as not to arouse suspicion. Obviously, a blank sheet of paper would give the game away!

Another substance useful for making invisible ink is nitrate of bismuth. When dry, a message written in a solution of this is quite invisible, but if the paper is wetted, the words stand out as dense white outlines.

It is not absolutely necessary to use chemicals for making an invisible ink, since a number of common liquids will work quite well. During the first Afghan War, for instance, a British officer in India received a message which seemed ordinary enough until he notice the word 'iodine' written at the bottom, which did not really make sense.

He sent for a bottle of iodine, and brushed the letter with the fluid, and, to his surprise, a second message appeared between the lines of the first. The sender of the letter had written another, secret message, using only rice-water, but when this was brushed with iodine, the words appeared plainly.

Another idea was used when smuggling a message into a prisoner's

Prisoner 'dusting' a secret message
written in milk

cell. The man's friends had written what appeared to be an ordinary letter, but in fact had added a second message between the lines, using ordinary milk as ink. The prisoner, receiving his letter, dirtied his finger on the dusty cell floor and then rubbed it over the message. The dirt stuck to the fatty content of the milk so bringing out the words of the secret writing.

Milk can also be used for messages which are held in front of a fire, so causing the letters to appear as brownish writing. Skimmed milk is best for this purpose, as creamy milk tends to produce fatty marks. Several other household liquids can be used for making invisible inks.

Onion juice works very well, but the onion can be used by itself, simply by stabbing a quill pen into the vegetable. The message will remain invisible until it is heated, when the words will appear in purple. Lemon, orange and grapefruit juice are all good invisible inks, and will produce brown writing after being heated.

Vinegar is also useful, but it is best to use the colourless kind, since ordinary brownish vinegar is liable to show up slightly. It is worth experimenting with some of the ordinary substances to be found in the kitchen. A teaspoonful of salt dissolved in a half-pint of water works well, and the same proportions can be used for sugar and honey. Washing soda, and Epsom salts can also be used.

All these inks are rendered visible by holding them near heat. A gas or electric fire is ideal, but an electric light bulb or hot electric iron will do. Do not let the paper, or fingers, get too near any naked flame or other form of heat. When concentrating on seeing the message appear, it would be easy to burn fingers, or let the paper catch fire. A spring clothes peg could be used to hold the paper, but it is far better to do any experiments of this kind under adult supervision.

How to Crack a Cipher

During the Second World War, Admiral Yamamoto, Commander-in-Chief of the Imperial Japanese Navy, made a special mission to a secret rendezvous somewhere in the Pacific. The Admiral was a qualified pilot, having led the famous attack on the U.S. Fleet at Pearl Harbour in 1941, so this time he was piloting his own bomber, which also contained several other high-ranking Japanese Staff officers.

Naturally, key Japanese positions were notified of the Admiral's flight, which was escorted by a squadron of Zero fighters. The top secret messages were sent out in what the Japanese believed to be an unbreakable secret cipher, but the radio signals were picked up by U.S. intelligence units, and relayed to Washington, where cipher experts got to work.

By the time Admiral Yamamoto and his staff had taken off, the Americans had cracked the cipher and the message was read by the War chiefs in Washington. Squadrons of Lockheed Lightnings from the USAAF sped out over the Pacific, sighting Yamamoto's bomber and escort near the Solomon Islands. The Japanese were taken completely by surprise, and minutes later, the Admiral's bomber was hurtling earthwards wreathed in flames, to explode as it smashed into the island of Bougainville.

It was a brilliant victory for the Americans, and a tribute to their cipher experts, who had broken what the Japanese had considered to be an 'unbreakable' cipher. It was not the first time that a nation had fallen into the error of believing they had invented such a thing.

Although almost all ciphers can be deciphered by experts, the easiest to work on are the simple substitution ciphers, in which every letter of the original message is replaced in the cipher version by the same letter throughout. In other words, A is always, say, D, B is always S, C is always R, and so on. Cipher experts have worked out 'frequency' tables, which show how often each letter of the alphabet occurs in ordinary sentences.

Of course, this is worked out on averages, since the frequency of letters is bound to vary from sentence to sentence, but it is surprising how often the tables are correct. The following list shows the letters of the alphabet in their order of frequency in the English language:

ET A O N R I S H D L F C M U G Y P W B V K X J Q Z

This shows that the most common letter in English is E, followed by T, A, O, and so on. In fact, E is very much more common than any of the others, and T follows very close behind. The letters can be grouped to show their frequencies:

Very common	Common	Next most common, in this order:	Less common
E	T	A O N R I S	H

Less common still	Much less common	Rarer
D L F C M U	G Y P W B	V K X J Q Z

Other frequency tables have been worked out for *pairs* of letters, in the order most commonly found in English:

TH HE AN RE ER IN ON AT ND ST ES EN OF TE ED OR TI HI AS TO AR OU IS IT
LE NT RI SE HA AL DE EA NE RO OM IO WE VE TA TR CO ME NG MA CE RA IC NS
UT US BE UN CH WA SI LA AD LI RT CA NC SO LL UR EL RS EM AC IM PR TT OT
WI EC

The most common words in English are:

THE OF AND TO IN A IS THAT FOR IT BY ARE BE WAS AS HE WITH HIS

On the following page is a sample cipher message to decipher, without knowing the key. It could be a substitution cipher, or be of the transposition type, but on examination, the letter-groupings seem to favour a substitution cipher.

Lockheed Lightnings in combat

SGBPB EPB E KTJDBP LU MBLMFB WEHSHKR ULP SGBHP
BKSPY MBPJHSQ ES SGB BKN LU SGHQ YBEP QSLM IEK SGBY
BKSBP SGB MLPSQ ES EK BEPFHBP NESB MFBEQB

The first thing to do is to make a chart of all the letters in the cipher,
which will show how often each letter occurs.

A		N	// 2
B	///////////////////// 21	O	
C		P	//////////// 12
D	/ 1	Q	///// 5
E	/////////// 11	R	/ 1
F	/// 3	S	/////////////// 15
G	////// 6	T	/ 1
H	////// 6	U	/// 3
I	/ 1	V	
J	// 2	W	/ 1
K	/////// 7	X	
L	////// 6	Y	/// 3
M	////// 6	Z	

The most common letter in the cipher is B, which occurs 21 times.
Looking back at the frequency table, the most common letter in
English is shown as E, therefore, B = E, and should be substituted
throughout the cipher:

??E?E ??E ? ????E? ?? ?E???E ??????? ??? ??E??
E???? ?E????? ?? ??E E?? ?? ???? ?E?? ???? ??? ??E?
E??E? ??E ????? ?? ?? E????E? ???E ??E??E

Three of the three-letter words in the cipher end in E. They are EPB,
and SGB (which occurs twice). The group SGB also occurs many
times in other words. The most common three-letter word in English,
according to the table, is THE, while TH is the most common two-
letter group. Assuming that SGB = THE, substitute T for S, and H
for G throughout the cipher:

THE?E ??E ? ????E? ?? ?E???E ???T??? ??? THE??
E?T?? ?E???T? ?T THE E?? ?? TH?? ?E?? ?T?? ??? THE?
E?TE? THE ???T? ?T ?? E????E? ??TE ??E??E

The first word looks very promising, since it could only be THERE
or THESE, and the third word could only be A or I. If P equalled S,
and E equalled I, the second word would read ISE, which makes no
sense. But if P = R, and E = A, the second word is ARE, and these
two letters should be substituted throughout:

THERE ARE A ????ER ?? ?E???E ?A?T??? ??R TH?R
E?TR? ?ER??T? AT THE E?? ?? TH?? ?EAR ?T?? ?A? THE?
E?TER THE ??RT? AT A? EAR ??ER ?ATE ??EA?E

Examining the remaining short words, first those with two letters,
the fifth word – in the cipher as LU – appears again later. The next most
common English word after THE is OF. The eighth word above is

ULP. P = R, so if LU = OF, then ULP should be FOR. Substituting further, the message now appears as:

THERE ARE A ????ER OF ?E???E ?A?T??? FOR THE?R
E?TR? ?ER??T? AT THE E?? OF TH?? ?EAR ?TO? ?A? THE?
E?TER THE ?ORT? AT A? EAR??ER ?ATE ??EA?E

According to the table, the most common English letters are E, T, A, O, N, R, I, and so on. E, T, A, O, R have already been deciphered but the letter N has not. It cannot be B, S, P, or E, since these letters are equivalent to E, T, R and A. The cipher letter appearing next most frequently is K, which might equal N. A glance at the partially-completed message shows that this fits quite well. Now THE?R is very likely THEIR, making H = I, ENTR? looks like ENTRY, making Y = Y, and EN? could easily be END, making N = D. Therefore, the message now reads:

THERE ARE A N???ER OF ?E???E ?AITIN? FOR THEIR
ENTRY ?ER ?IT? AT THE END OF THI? YEAR ?TO?
?AN THEY ENTER THE ?ORT? AT AN EAR?IER DATE ??EA?E

It would seem that the last letter of ?AITIN? could be G, the last letter of THI? could be S, and the missing letter from EAR?IER could be L, making R = G, Q = S, and F = L:

THERE ARE A N???ER OF ?E??LE ?AITING FOR THEIR
ENTRY ?ER?ITS AT THE END OF THIS YEAR STO?
?AN THEY ENTER THE ?ORTS AT AN EARLIER DATE ?LEASE

From the sense of the message so far deciphered, it is now possible to guess the remaining letters. ?ER?ITS must be PERMITS, making M = P, and J = M. If thiis so, then ?E??LE is now PE?PLE, obviously PEOPLE, making L = O. The message now reads as follows:

THERE ARE A NUMBER OF PEOPLE WAITING FOR THEIR
ENTRY PERMITS AT THE END OF THIS YEAR STOP
CAN THEY ENTER THE PORTS AT AN EARLIER DATE PLEASE

Making out a table of the equivalent letters, the cipher appears as follows:

Cipher	E	D	I	N	B	U	R	G	H	a	c	F	J
'Clear'	A	B	C	D	E	F	G	H	I	J	K	L	M

Cipher	K	L	M	o	P	Q	S	T	v	W	x	Y	z
'Clear'	N	O	P	Q	R	S	T	U	V	W	X	Y	Z

Although some letters did not appear in the cipher message, it is possible to see that this was a simple substitution cipher of the 'Julius Caesar' type, having the keyword EDINBURGH. The letters shown in lower case letters were not used in the cipher, but it is possible to tell their equivalents from the positions of other letters in the alphabet.

Some Cipher Problems

1. Here is a message written in what looks like Russian. Can you work it out?

   Пусикат, пусикат, уэр хав ю бин?
   Аив бин уп ту Лондон ту визит зе куин.

2. Another 'alphabet' problem. Do you think this is written in Greek or English?

   Ω Μηρι, θιο Λονδονσ α υονδαφυλ σαιτ,
   Υιθ θε πιπλαλ υερκινγ βαι δε ανδ βαι ναιτ.

3. If you were a Gypsy, you could read this easily!

   ⊖ΙΒ ⊖ҍᗰᗷᑲ⊤ ⊙Βꓷ,
   ΙΒ ᴧΒᴧ⊤ ⊙Ρꓷ,
   ꓷⵔΒ ▷Βᗰꓷ ᗰᗷΒ ꓷ⊤Βꓷⵔⵔ⊙
   Βᴧ ᗰᗷΒ ▷▷ꓷ.

4. If you cannot understand this, a glance at page 30 will give you a clue.

   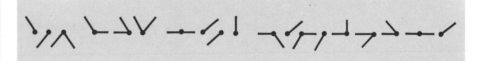

5. Here is a transposition cipher, rather like that on page 37. The keyword is STANDBY:

   AEGNCHT GRAUHED BKCUATI HPMANGA CYBELAT
   OOLCWOC OYADKTX

6. If you have made a grille like that shown on page 39, you should be able to work out the transposition cipher on the left.

   ```
   R R T E S R I E E Q
   U N E C R O N S I D
   F R E A D S S O O A
   R O S M Y T R I C O
   E N P M E A N A S T
   S D S P S O S U A S
   R I V B R I S O R E
   H L E U R U G N D E
   E E E A D N Q U E D
   A T N N D A D L Y S
   ```

7. This is a substitution cipher. Remember how Julius Caesar designed his? Then you should be able to decipher this one, using the keyword EXACTLY. You may like to refer back to page 44.
   Here is the cipher problem:

   QUESTION: UEP DQ E OEQ D PEU?
   ANSWER: JK, IDPP, DQ DP PDIKJ!

8. King Solomon knew all about the characters on page 71, since he invented them! Can you work this out? You can refer to page 44.

On page 45, page 48, page 49, page 53, page 60, page 66

9. On page 45, we describe the cipher invented by Giovanni Porta. Here is a message in this cipher, using the keyword WEALTH:

AYPSQ BQDKB ZJWQV AVNMB RFPSB JBJNK VHKDI

10. Porta's queer symbol cipher appears on page 48, and on the right is a message written in it.

11. Blaise de Vigenère's cipher is described on page 49. See if you can work out this cipher message, using the keyword UNTIDY:

CJXVW YBHGB LLABG BKCJY TQQQ
NUXXO YCALW IRCZU CFRIB
BAKMN BGMES WXYWU YFYFG SYCAL
IQBBR PIVYM YBUES WXMWR

12. If you have made the cipher-wheel described on page 53, you can decipher this message, with the key-number 1066:

TBNCW JMYEC XDTCF QLFSB XBSYS REBTQY
FHERO HLRCX IBAWYU
MTFHJ WWMFN GMRPG MYWRB IHVSF NG
MYWRB IHVSM MYUBX QYBZF UU

13. Here is a cipher-problem worked out in the Playfair cipher, which is described on page 60. The keyword is NATURE:

NFMFO EGFAM CTAJB DNFCM GTLMA TKG
AJTUG FNWFM PCPZZ SGPDN QPTGR PUNTH IZ
GFCPA CFMTH CUOBA XGBNF WQNYB CCVGE
WQRKB ECTAJ BETBB MERTU RNBDG FTA

14. Finally, here is a cipher message for you to decipher without knowing anything about it. It is quite a simple one, and a glance at page 66 should help you:

RDE EVQFEQR LFNDEPQ RM UM VPE RDMQE WFRD
RDE TEPY QFJNIE LDVKCEQ VKU WDEK MKE IERREP
FQ VIWVYQ PENIVLEU AY MKE MRDEP IERREP

Answers

Ogham cipher, p.13:
   SEND HELP AT ONCE.
Ogham cipher, p.13:
   MEET ME AT THE CROSSROADS.
Acrostic, p.37:
   THE CAT AND THE FIDDLE.
Letter, p.39:
   THIS MAN IS A SPY DO NOT TRUST SHOOT HIM.
Chinese cipher, p.45:
   TOP SECRET.
Freemason's cipher, p.46:
   TREASURE ISLAND BY ROBERT LOUIS STEVENSON.
Baconian cipher, p.52:
   BACON DID NOT WRITE THIS PLAY IT WAS
   SHAKESPEARE.
Shopkeeper's code, p.56:
   £5.50.
'Dancing men' cipher, p.57:
   PLEASE COME AT ONCE.
Musical cipher, p.60:
   THE SOUND OF MUSIC.
Cipher problems, see page 70:

1. Phonetically, the message will look like this in Latin letters:
    PUSIKAT, PUSIKAT, UER KHAV YU BIN?
    AIV BIN UP TU LONDON TU VIZIT ZE KUIN.
    Or, in proper English:
    PUSSYCAT, PUSSYCAT, WHERE HAVE YOU BEEN?
    I'VE BEEN UP TO LONDON TO VISIT THE QUEEN.

2. The message is written in Greek characters, and phonetically, would
    look like this:
    O MERI, THIS LONDONS A UONDAPHUL SAIT,
    UITH THE PIPL AL UERKING BAI DE AND BAI NAIT.
    And, in proper English:
    Oh Mary, this London's a wonderful sight,
    With the people all working by day and by night.

3. The Gypsy alphabet would be put into the Latin alphabet some-
    thing like this:
    MAI MOTHER SED   (MY MOTHER SAID)
    AI NEVR SHUD   (I NEVER SHOULD)
    PLE UITH THE DJIPSIS (PLAY WITH THE GYPSIES)
    IN THE UUD   (IN THE WOOD)

4. This is the semaphore alphabet, adapted as a cipher:
    CAN YOU READ SEMAPHORE?

5. The keyword is STANDBY. So, to decipher, you must first
    rearrange the letters of STANDBY in alphabetical order:
    ABDNSTY. Then write this over the top, and arrange the groups
    of the cipher like this, beneath:

A B D N S T Y
A E G N C H T
G R A U H E D
B K C U A T I
H P M A N G A
C Y B E L A T
O O L C W O C
O Y A D K T X

S T A N D B Y
C H A N G E T
H E G U A R D
A T B U C K I
N G H A M P A
L A C E B Y T
W O O C L O C
K T O D A Y X

Now place the letters of the keyword back into the correct order, and also move each column of letters with it:

Reading across the block, you have CHANGET HEGUARD ATBUCKI NGHAMPA LACEBYT WOOCLOC KTODAYX, which correctly spaced out, should read: CHANGE THE GUARD AT BUCKINGHAM PALACE BY TWO O'CLOCK TODAY. The last X is, of course, a null. ·

6. Message reads: SECOND ARMY IS SURROUNDED AND REINFORCEMENTS ARE URGENTLY REQUIRED STOP ADVISE HEADQUARTERS AS SOON AS POSSIBLE—ENDS.

7. The keyword should be written over the alphabet like this:

E X A C T L Y B D F G H I J K M N O P Q R S U V W Z
A B C D E F G H I J K L M N O P Q R S T U V W X Y Z

This gives the answer to the cipher as follows:
QUESTION: WAS IT A RAT I SAW?
ANSWER: NO, MISS, IT IS SIMON!
Now read each sentence backwards, and see what happens!

8. King Solomon's cipher problem should read like this:

> Like a grate full of coals I burn,
> A great, full house to see;
> And if I should not grateful prove,
> A great fool I should be.

9. The keyword for Porta's cipher should be written along the top of the cipher message like this:

W E A L T H W E A L T H W E A L T H W E A L T H W E A L T H
A Y P S Q B Q D K B Z J W Q V A V N M B R F P S B J B J N K

W E A L T
V H K D I

Look in the first upright column for W, which shares a row with X. The first letter of the cipher is A, which, in the 'WX' row, stands above P. P is the first letter of the 'clear' message. Next letter of the keyword is E, which appears in the first upright column as 'EF'. The cipher letter is Y, which stands below A in the 'EF' row. A is the second letter of the 'clear' message. Continuing until the 'clear' message is completed: PACK MY BOX WITH FIVE DOZEN LIQUOR JUGS (followed by the three nulls, X, Y and Z). This sentence contains all the letters of the alphabet.

10. Porta's symbol cipher should read:

> Among our numerous English rhymes,
> They say there's none for 'month';
> I tried and failed a hundred times,
> But succeeded the hundred and 'onth'.

11. The Vigenère cipher should be deciphered like this. Write the keyword UNTIDY over the top of the cipher message, repeated over and over again:

```
U N T I D Y U N T I D Y U N T I D Y U N T I D Y
C J X V W Y B H G B L L A B G B K C J Y T Q Q Q
U N T I D Y U N T I D Y U N T I D Y U N
N U X X O Y Ç A L W I R C Z U C F R I B

T I D Y U N T I D Y U N T I D Y U N T I D Y U N T
B A K M N B G M X S W X Y W U Y F Y F G S Y C A L

I D Y U N T I D Y U N T I D Y U N T I D
I Q B B R P I V Y M Y B U E S W X M W R
```

The first step is to look down the first vertical column for the first letter of the keyword, which is U. Now run along the horizontal row, and look for C, the first letter of the cipher message. The top letter of the C column is in capital letters, and is I, which is the first letter of the 'clear' message. Next keyword letter is N. Below it, in the cipher, is J. Look for J in the N row, and then look to the top of the N column, and find the capital letter, and find the letter W. Next keyword letter is T, and in the T row, look for cipher-letter X, and at the top of the X row is E. Now you have IWE. Continue in this way through the cipher-message, which should finally read like this:

> I WENT A-HUNTING ON THE PLAINS,
> THE PLAINS OF TIMBUCTOO;
> I SHOT ONE BUCK FOR ALL MY PAINS,
> AND HE WAS A SLIM BUCK, TOO!

12. The cipher-wheel message should read:

> HIS DEATH, WHICH HAPPENED IN HIS BERTH
> AT FORTY-ODD BEFELL.
> THEY WENT AND TOLD THE SEXTON, AND
> THE SEXTON TOLLED THE BELL!

13. The Playfair cipher message should be deciphered as:

> RESEMBLE NOT THE CREEPING SNAIL
> THAT LEAVES ITS SLIME UPON ITS TRAIL.
> LET IT BE SAID, THAT WHERE YOU'VE BEEN
> YOU LEFT THE FACE OF NATURE CLEAN!

Remember, the Playfair box, using the NATURE keyword, should look like this:

```
N A T U R
E B C D F
G H IJ K L
M O P Q S
V W X Y Z
```

14. Cipher-message for deciphering: Note that letter E in the cipher occurs 20 times, far more than any other. So it is possible that E = E. Next is R, with 11 occurences. So probably R = T (check the frequency table on page 66). The first group of letters RDE is probably T ?E – most likely THE. Substitute throughout message, and the first stage is completed. Final message reads: THE EASIEST CIPHERS TO DO ARE THOSE WITH THE VERY SIMPLE CHANGES AND WHEN ONE LETTER IS ALWAYS REPLACED BY ONE OTHER LETTER. Set out, this produces the following:

```
V A L U E B C D f g h I J K M N o P Q R s T W x Y z
A B C D E F G H I J K L M N O P Q R S T U V W X Y Z
```

The lower case letters do not appear in the cipher-message, but can be worked out from those which do appear.

HOW TO MAKE THE CIPHER-WHEEL

This is the way to make the cipher-wheel described on page 53. Trace the two discs, and transfer on to thin card (an old cereal packet will do). When the paste is dry, carefully cut out the discs, and place the smaller disc on top of the larger one. Now push a drawing-pin through the very centre of each disc. You can bend the point of the pin over, or else you can push the point into a piece of cork or rubber eraser.

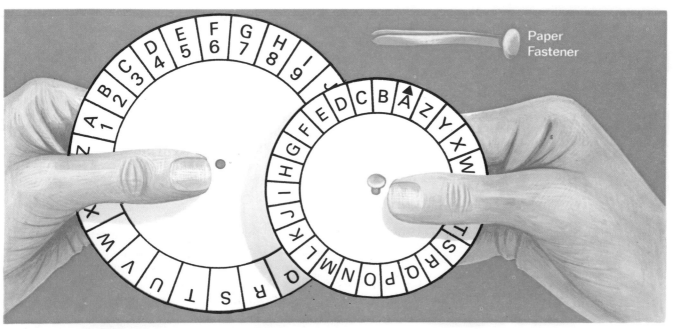

Index